William Hoyle

Our national resources and how they are wasted

An omitted chapter in political economy

William Hoyle

Our national resources and how they are wasted
An omitted chapter in political economy

ISBN/EAN: 9783337134457

Printed in Europe, USA, Canada, Australia, Japan

Cover: Foto ©Suzi / pixelio.de

More available books at **www.hansebooks.com**

OUR NATIONAL RESOURCES;

AND HOW THEY ARE WASTED.

AN OMITTED CHAPTER IN POLITICAL ECONOMY.

BY

WILLIAM HOYLE,

Author of "An Enquiry into the Causes of the Long Continued Depression in the Cotton Trade," &c. &c.

LONDON: SIMPKIN, MARSHALL, & CO.
MANCHESTER: JOHN HEYWOOD, 141 AND 143, DEANSGATE.

CONTENTS.

CHAP.		PAGE.
I.	On the Development of our Manufacturing Industry	1
II.	On the Sources of our National Wealth	15
III.	On Pauperism	37
IV.	On the Falling Off in Trade	43
V.	Productive and Non-productive Labour and Expenditure	53
VI.	On the Main Cause of Bad Trade and National Waste	97
VII.	On the Right Expenditure of Money	107
VIII.	The Remedy	131

PREFACE.

THE attention of the writer of the following pages was first specially directed to the subject treated therein, in the autumn of 1868.

During the whole of the years 1867 and 1868, the trade of the United Kingdom, but especially the cotton trade, was in a most depressed condition. The year 1869 was ushered in; but, instead of there being an improvement, so far at least as the cotton trade went, matters grew worse. The belief at that time was almost universal in Lancashire, that the depressed condition of trade arose from the fact that our continental neighbours were outstripping us in manufacturing, and that they were still more certain to outstrip us in the future; and, consequently, the great cotton trade of Lancashire would shortly be a thing of the past. Having a considerable interest at stake, the author, like other spinners and manufacturers, naturally became anxious about this unpleasant prospect, and, therefore, during the winter of 1868-9 he spent his leisure evenings in giving the subject a careful investigation. In the autumn of 1869, the results of this investigation were embodied and published by him in a pamphlet, entitled, "An Enquiry into the Cause of the Present Long-Continued Depression in the Cotton Trade, with Suggestions for its Improvement." The investigation entirely disabused the mind of the author of all those ideas, as to the falling off of our foreign trade owing to continental competition, and the publication of the pamphlet did much to allay the fears of the commercial classes in reference to the matter. An examination of our exports of manufactured goods, alike in cotton, woollen, and linen, showed that a continued and enormous increase had taken place, and that the depression in trade arose from the falling off in the home trade. To show this, and to exhibit the cause for this falling off, was the author's object in publishing the pamphlet to which reference has been made. The present volume is an attempt to give the question a more general and extended investigation, and, at the same time, to some extent, to treat of kindred questions, such as productive and non-productive labour, and expenditure, questions which are but very imperfectly comprehended, but mistakes in regard to which, often have a most injurious influence, in depressing our trade and wasting our national resources.

The purpose of the author in the following treatise, therefore, is—

1st. To show that the inventions and improvements in machinery by our countrymen, have given to us exceptional facilities for the acquisition of wealth.

2nd. That these facilities are very much enhanced in their value, by other important material advantages which we possess.

3rd. That, aided by these facilities, our trade and commerce have been developed into enormous proportions; and that our opportunities for getting wealth have increased in a corresponding degree.

4th. That the commercial depression which has existed during the last few years, has not resulted from any falling off in our Foreign Trade, but from a considerable decrease in the Home Trade.

5th. That this decrease has arisen mainly, if not entirely, from the improvident and unproductive character of our labour and expenditure, especially in reference to the article of intoxicating drinks.

6th. That notwithstanding our vast facilities for obtaining wealth, a large class of our population are constantly sunk in pauperism and destitution.

7th. That if our labour were properly directed, and our expenditure properly applied, settled pauperism or destitution could not possibly exist.

In the treatment of this question, the author has carefully guarded against quoting any statistics, or stating any fact, that did not appear to be of undisputed authority. The statistics given are, in most cases, taken from Government returns, and in all instances reference is made to the authority, so that if the reader wishes to check the quotations for himself he can do so. In many points, where there are no published or known data, the author has had to give the best estimate he could, according to his own experience and judgment. In no case, however, do these estimates affect the argument, unless it be in degree. This the reader will be good enough to bear in mind, and where he thinks the quantities assumed are too great or too small, let him apply the argument to such data as may appear to him more correct.

To those readers who have paid much attention to the subject, it may seem that some questions are treated too much in detail, and, also, that the writer has been guilty of repetition. If these faults should appear, they arise partly from intention and partly from want of time. The reader will, however, observe, whenever there may appear to be a repetition, the argument is generally presented in a somewhat different form to what it was before. Some of the topics have appeared so important to the author that it seemed desirable to present them to the reader's mind in different places and associations; he has also laboured to be as plain and homely as possible in the illustrations; and if by this, conviction has been produced, the author will be very glad to forego all pretension to merit in the composition, for the hope of making an impression upon his readers.

It may be that some who read this treatise, may be disappointed that the investigation and the argument have not been extended to other causes of national waste. When the investigation was begun, it was the author's intention thus to extend the inquiry; but the questions involved were so numerous, and generally so insignificant in comparison to the one treated of, that the resolution was abandoned.

The intelligent reader, however, will readily apply the argument to other topics, and thereby, without adding to its bulk, the usefulness of the book will be increased.

Tottington, near Bury,
  Lancashire, February 6th, 1871.

CHAPTER I.*

ON THE DEVELOPMENT OF OUR MANUFACTURING INDUSTRY.

Sources of our wealth.

IN order that a full idea may be gathered as to the present position of our national resources, it will be needful briefly to enumerate the principal sources from whence our wealth is derived. These may be summed up as follows :—

1st. Manufactures and Commerce.

2nd. Agriculture.

3rd. Mines, Railways, and other description of property.

Mechanical advantages.

The extent of our manufacturing advantages cannot be fully appreciated, unless we take into consideration their origin and rapid development as influenced by the introduction of machinery, &c.; and as our different industries have all of

---

* For the facts contained in this chapter, the author is mainly indebted to Mr. J. A. Mann's "History of the Cotton Trade," published by Simpkin, Marshall, and Co.; Dr. John Watts's "History of the Cotton Famine," published by Simpkin, Marshall, and Co.; and the chapters on National Industry in the "Pictorial History of England," published by W. and R. Chambers, of Edinburgh and London.

them very greatly participated in the advantages derived from these mechanical inventions, the history of one will therefore substantially be the history of all. In order, therefore, to illustrate this, I will give a brief account of the development of the cotton trade.

When the enormous magnitude of our trade and commerce is considered, and contrasted with its condition a hundred years ago, it becomes a subject full of interest to consider the various steps by which this development has been accomplished.

Our industries a century ago and now.

The entire exports of the United Kingdom for the whole of the ten years ending 1769, amounted in value to £157,052,626, whilst for the year 1869 alone they amounted to £190,045,230, or upwards of thirty millions more in value for one year than during ten years a century ago.

According to Mr. J. A. Mann, the entire exports of cotton goods in the year 1751 amounted in value only to £45,986, whilst in 1869 the value of cotton goods exported was £67,159,064.

Protection in former times.

The backward condition of our manufacturing industry one hundred years ago may be judged of, when it is remembered that at that time we imported considerable quantities of goods from India, in the face of a protective duty of 4d. in the pound, which, after the fashion of those days, was thought essential to the prosperity of our manufactures; whilst, at the same time, there were prohibitions imposed upon cotton goods from other countries. The protection thus afforded did not, however, bring about the desired result, for it is stated that in 1757 the total annual value of our cotton manufactures did not amount to more than £200,000. *(margin: CHAP. I. Its results.)*

In the year 1743 commenced those improvements, which have continued to progress, and which have resulted in the present expansion of our manufacturing industries. It was in this year that John Kay, of Bury, invented the fly-shuttle and picking-peg. Before his time the weaver, in order to work his shuttle, had to stretch his arms from side to side of the loom, and if the cloth were more than 36 inches wide it needed two persons to do this, one being unable to reach across the loom. Kay's invention consisted in making the lathe in which the shuttle runs about 18 inches longer, so as to permit of a shuttle-box on each side of the cloth, and then, by means of a string fastened to the picker on each side of the loom, and joined to a handle in the middle, the weaver was enabled to work the shuttle from the centre. A great loss in time was thus avoided, and, where wide cloth had to be woven, one person, by the aid of these improvements, could do the work formerly done by two. *(margin: Commencement of mechanical improvements. John Kay's invention.)*

In the year 1769, Robert Kay, the son of the above John Kay, invented the drop-box. This invention consisted in constructing the shuttle-box so that it would rise or fall, and enable the weaver, when using alternately different kinds of weft, to *(margin: Robert Kay's invention.)*

keep his loom at work; whereas, previously, he had had to stop his loom to change the shuttles. A great saving of time was in this way effected, and the out-turn of work materially expedited.

James Hargreaves and the spinning-jenny.

In the year 1767, or thereabouts, James Hargreaves, a poor weaver of Blackburn, conceived the idea of the spinning-jenny. Before his time, one person could only tend one spindle and spin one thread at a time. By means of the jenny, one hand was enabled to work twenty or thirty spindles at once, and thus turn off an immensely greater quantity of work than formerly.

Richard Arkwright and the water-frame.

In 1769, Richard Arkwright, of Preston, invented what is generally termed the water-frame, or, as it is sometimes called, the throstle-frame. This was an application of rollers to the stretching of the yarn, so as to regulate the counts (or thickness of the thread) uniformly, and stretch the yarn with precision, these rollers being so arranged as to work in connection with the spindle.

Samuel Crompton and the mule.

In the year 1779, Samuel Crompton, of Bolton, combined Hargreaves's jenny with Arkwright's rollers, and thus brought out the mule. Through the skill of Mr. Roberts, of Manchester, the mule was made self-acting, the spinner not having now to work or guide the mule, but simply to see to its being kept in order. The value of these accumulated inventions will be seen when it is remembered that, as has been stated, before the invention of Hargreaves, one person could only tend one spindle; at the present time, one man, aided by a grown-up youth and boy, will tend a pair of mules having 1,200 or 1,300 spindles in each, or 2,600 spindles altogether. If these facts be carefully examined, it will be seen that one individual, aided by the machinery of the present day, will produce as much yarn as seven hundred and fifty persons could have done little over one hundred years ago.

Labour economised by the mule.

From these improvements there has resulted,

1st. A large diminution in the cost of yarn, and

2nd. A considerable increase of wages.

According to Mr. Mann, a spinner in 1760 could only earn from 2s. to 3s. weekly; whereas, now, he can earn from 30s. to 35s. weekly. In the time of Crompton, which was after considerable improvements had been made in machinery, the cost of spinning weft, 40 hanks to the pound, was 14s. per pound; for No. 60's 25s. per pound; and for No. 80's 42s. per pound. Now, the respective cost of producing will be, 40's 4d.; for 60's 7½d.; and for 80's 1s. per pound.* Such are the advantages resulting from the invention of machinery.

Wages in 1760.

Cost of spinning yarn.

These important improvements in spinning machinery were quickly followed by a largely

---

* For the information of those who are not conversant with manufacturing phraseology, it may be stated that a hank contains 810 yards and that when "counts of yarn" are spoken of, the number of hanks it takes to weigh a pound is meant. Thus, by 60's yarn is meant yarn of which it takes 60 hanks, each of 810 yards, to weigh one pound.

Increased production by spinning machinery.

increased production of yarn, so much so, as somewhat to glut the market. At a meeting in Manchester, in 1784, it was urged that it would be impossible to find hands to weave all the yarn which would be spun.* Dr. Cartwright argued that the same excellency might be arrived at in weaving, as had been attained in spinning; but he was met by a decided contradiction. He, however, undauntedly set to work, and the result was a very rude model of the power-loom, which was afterwards (in 1813) perfected and brought into general use by Mr. Horrocks, of Stockport.

These inventions, important as they were, would have been very much restricted in their use had it not been that other inventions and discoveries were made simultaneously with them.

Motive power in former times.

On the first establishment of mills, the machinery was either driven by cattle or turned by human labour. This continued for some considerable time. By-and-bye mills, began to be erected in the neighbourhood of waterfalls; these, however, were very limited, and often very inconveniently situated. What was wanted was such arrangements as would enable manufacturers to carry the machinery into the towns and villages where the people dwelt; and not to be obliged to put down their mills at outside places, in order to secure turning power by means of the waterfalls, which often necessitated long journeys, the con-

---

* See Mann's History of the Cotton Trade, page 17.

struction of new roads, and many other inconveniences, involving such an amount of cost and trouble as proved most serious obstacles to the establishment of mills.

In 1765, the genius of Watt produced the steam-engine. Previous to Watt's time there had been a kind of engine in use, generally styled Newcomen's engine; but it was very rude and imperfect, and required such an enormous amount of fuel to drive it as to make it excessively costly. The motion, too, of this engine was very irregular, and thereby totally unfitted for the turning of machinery: hence its use was mainly restricted to the pumping of water out of the Cornish and Newcastle mines. Watt applied the condenser to the steam-engine; he also arranged the valves so that the steam was turned upon each end of the piston, instead of upon one end as heretofore. He also made many other alterations and additions, which greatly tended to improve the working of the engine, to reduce the cost of fuel, and to secure the regularity which was needed for the efficient working of machinery.

James Watt and the steam-engine.

To show the enormous saving of fuel effected by Watt's engine, it may be stated that the proprietor of the Chacewater Mines, in Cornwall, put down three of Watt's engines; and the saving in coal was so great that he agreed to pay to Watt £800 per annum, per engine, for the benefit thus received.*

Economy of Watt's engine.

---

* See Pictorial History of England, vol. v., page 476.

CHAP. I.

Reduction of labour and cost by machinery.

James Brindley and the canal system.

It has been pointed out, that the invention of the steam-engine simultaneously with that of the machinery for manufacturing, was a coincidence fraught with the most important results.

If these inventions did not altogether annihilate physical labour, they reduced it to a minimum, and they led to the introduction of the factory system, by which a thorough subdivision of labour was secured, increased skill developed, a large amount of time thereby saved, and a vast reduction effected in the cost of production.

Whilst these improvements in machinery were going on, other discoveries were being effected, which materially aided the success of our manufacturing industries. Six years before Watt invented the steam-engine, the celebrated Brindley had completed the first canal from Worsley to Manchester. This so much reduced the cost in the carriage of coal, as to lower the price of coal in Manchester by one-half. The construction of this canal was followed, six years later, by that of the Grand Trunk Canal, whereby the clays of Devonshire, &c., were carried at a cheap rate to the Potteries, thereby greatly reducing the cost of the earthenware manufactured in those districts. Other canals were rapidly constructed, new and good roads were also made, which very much facilitated and cheapened the cost of transit, thereby aiding very materially the development of our manufactures and trade.

In 1764, the art of calico printing was introduced

into Lancashire, and gave a considerable impetus to the cotton industry. A further stimulus was given to it by the discovery and application of chlorine in the process of bleaching, which was introduced from France by James Watt, the inventor of the steam-engine, and applied at the works of his father-in-law, Mr. MacGregor, of Glasgow. Before the application of this discovery, nearly all the cotton goods, in order to be bleached, had to be taken to Holland, where they lay for five or six months in the open air in the fields around Haarlem. When we remember the difficulty of transit in those days, it will be at once seen what a drawback it must have been, to have to take cotton goods manufactured in Lancashire all the way to Holland to be bleached, involving enormous expense, and losing the greater portion of a year in the process. At the present time, the bleaching of calicoes can be effected in as many days as it formerly took months, and is done more effectually also.

Prior to the inventions of Hargreaves, Arkwright, Crompton, Watt, &c., the operations of spinning and weaving were entirely carried on by people at their own homes. As machinery came into use, and trade became more extended, the factory system came into existence. This, as has been pointed out, enabled the manufacturer to effect a thorough subdivision of labour; each man thereby became expert at his particular work, doing more of it, and doing it better and at less cost than before the introduction of machinery.

One considerable drawback in the first establishment of factories, especially during the long winter nights, was the cost and danger arising from the lighting up of the mills. This had to be done by means of candles, which were not only very costly, but full of danger arising from the sparks which were perpetually emitted from the candles. The writer was informed a short time ago, by a gentleman whose ancestors were in the cotton trade upwards of sixty years ago, that the cost of candles during the winter months in those days was almost equal to the cost of cotton. These difficulties, however, were overcome by the discovery and application of gas, which was first applied in 1802, by Mr. Murdoch, of the Soho Works, Birmingham. In 1802 the first cotton mill in Salford was lighted up with gas, and the practice was rapidly extended to all other mills.

The limits of this treatise will not permit me to dwell in detail, or even to specify more than a few of the other improvements which have occurred, in addition to those already enumerated. Among other things may be mentioned the application of steam to propelling ships, which was first accomplished by Bell, in 1811; the construction of the locomotive engine by Stephenson, in 1814; the establishment of the railway system, first begun by the construction of the Stockton and Darlington Railway in 1824, and fully completed by the opening of the Manchester and Liverpool line, in 1830; the application of electricity to telegraphy, by Wheatstone and Cooke, in 1837; and other inventions too numerous to specify. Suffice it to say, that the inventions of the last hundred years have completely revolutionized the manufactures and commerce of the world, and have placed in our hands a monopoly of trade and wealth such as has never been enjoyed by any nation in the history of the world. How long we may maintain this position depends upon the manner in which we use the advantages we thus possess.

Our advantages.

We not only possess immense advantages from the superiority of our machinery, but also in many other ways we enjoy facilities for production which other nations are destitute of.

Climate.

1st. Our climate is well adapted for manufacturing. Those who are engaged in cotton manufacturing are well aware of the vast advantages which are derived from a suitable climate. The differences produced in manufacturing between a dry east wind and a westerly one, amounts to at least five per cent., both in quantity and quality, that is, if when a westerly wind blows, a mill containing one thousand looms, manufactures weekly four thousand pieces of cloth, that same mill, if the wind blows from the east for a week, will not produce more than three thousand eight hundred pieces, or even less than that, and what it does produce will not be so good.

East wind; its pernicious influence.

This arises from the fact that a moist climate is best adapted to the working of the cotton staples; a dry atmosphere makes the yarn tender and brittle; and hence the breezes which blow from our western shores, which are washed by the equatorial current from the Gulf of Mexico, &c., partake exactly of the characteristic most needed for manufacturing. These remarks apply also, to a considerable extent, to the manufacture of woollens and other fabrics.

Coal, &c.

2nd. Our mineral resources, too, are highly favourable for manufacturing. Were it not for the plentiful supply of good coal which we possess, we should be unable to obtain the large quantities of fuel which are needed to supply our steam engines. In this country, coal is not only abundant but it is good, and it is found in the immediate locality where our mills are situated. On the Continent, in those districts which possess coal, it is very inferior, and often inconveniently situated; so that manufacturers are frequently obliged either to carry their own coal long distances, or else import them from this country.

Our insular position.

3rd. We possess immense advantages also in point of situation. The insular character of our country, too, is of immense advantage, as it gives us a ready approach to the sea on all sides. We have also many and excellent harbours; and, as no place is very far from the seaboard, the cost of carriage becomes trifling, and the conveniences for shipping such as greatly to facilitate commerce, whether inward or outward.

Secret of our progress.

A perusal of this chapter will convince the reader that the development and progress of our manufacturing industry, during the last 100 years, has been something surpassing by far all the progress made in the previous history of the world. This progress has been mainly, if not entirely, owing to the genius and discoveries of our own countrymen; and it has given to us such a precedence as largely to place in our hands a monopoly of the manufacturing industries of the world.

The invention of the steam-engine simultaneously with that of the machinery for manufactures, supplied us with mechanical power by which to turn our mills; the vast deposits of iron and coal underlying the soil in most parts of our island, give us the material from which to construct our machinery, and also the necessary fuel to develop the motive power for the working of the steam-engine; the construction of canals, roads, railways, &c., has enabled us quickly and cheaply to transport our goods from one part to another; and when, in addition to this, we remember that our climate is the one best adapted for manufacturing, and that our people are among the most industrious and persevering of the nations of the world, it will be clearly seen that we have enjoyed, and still enjoy, facilities for manufacturing, and consequently for the accumulation of wealth, such as are not, and never have been, possessed by any other nation upon the face of the earth; and such as, had they been properly husbanded and used, would have placed us as a nation in circumstances far beyond the reach of pauperism or destitution.

Some of these advantages are the bountiful gifts of the Creator, and are not likely to fail us in the future. Others, involving questions of national character and conduct, are largely dependent upon the manner in which our extended resources are employed. If rightly used, these will tend to the nation's elevation ; but if misapplied, they are sure to lead to its demoralization, and ultimately to its downfall.

CHAPTER II.

ON THE SOURCES OF OUR NATIONAL WEALTH.

THE main sources from which our national wealth is derived are the following :—

1st. Manufactures.

2nd. Trade and Commerce.

3rd. Agriculture.

4th. Mines, Railways, Fisheries, &c.

MANUFACTURES.—Some idea may be formed of the magnitude of our manufactures from the following table of mills engaged therein. It is taken from a return presented to both Houses of Parliament, July 22nd, 1868.

Return of mills engaged in textile manufactures.

RETURN OF THE NUMBER OF MILLS ENGAGED IN TEXTILE MANUFACTURES.

	No. of Mills.	No. of Spindles.	No. of Looms.	No. of Horse Power	No. of Hands Employed.
Cotton	2,549	32,000,014	379,329	201,062	401,064
Woollen	2,465	6,456,989	118,865	87,623	253,087
Linen	405	1,588,124	31,040	46,866	118,929
Other Kinds (incl. Silk)	1,003	1,072,467	20,131	17,544	75,707
	6,422	41,117,594	549,365	353,095	848,787

When it is borne in mind that, 120 years ago, machinery, except such as was worked by hand

Machinery unknown 120 years ago.

and of the rudest kind, was altogether unknown, and that such a thing as a mill of the modern kind was not in existence, it will give an idea as to the progress we have made, and the vast facilities which machinery has given us for the accumulation of wealth. Our country has to a great extent been the workshop of the world, and has reaped a rich harvest of wealth as a consequence.

TRADE AND COMMERCE.—No better proof can be given of the giant strides made in our trade and commerce, than a comparison of our present foreign trade with what it was a hundred years ago. The following tables will illustrate this:—

TABLE OF IMPORTS AND EXPORTS FOR EACH OF THE TEN YEARS ENDING 1769.*

	Imports. £	Exports. £
1760	10,683,596	15,781,176
1761	10,292,541	16,038,913
1762	9,579,160	14,543,336
1763	12,568,927	15,578,943
1764	11,250,660	17,446,306
1765	11,812,144	15,763,868
1766	12,456,765	15,188,669
1767	13,097,153	15,090,001
1768	13,116,281	16,620,132
1769	13,134,091	15,001,282
	117,991,318	157,052,626

* See McCulloch's Commercial Dictionary, page 726.

Table of Imports and Exports for each of the ten years ending 1869.*

	Imports.	Exports.
	£	£
1860	210,530,873	135,891,227
1861	217,485,024	125,102,814
1862	225,716,976	123,992,264
1863	248,919,020	146,602,342
1864	274,952,172	160,449,053
1865	271,072,285	165,835,725
1866	295,290,274	188,917,536
1867	275,183,137	180,961,923
1868	294,693,608	179,677,812
1869	295,428,967	190,045,230
	2,609,272,336	1,597,475,926

Our foreign trade for the ten years ending 1869.

In the year 1770, the population of the United Kingdom was estimated at 11,198,276; in the present year, 1870, it is estimated to be 30,838,210; or, whilst our population has only doubled itself two and three-quarter times over, our imports (which are an index of the growth of our national wealth) have increased twenty-two fold.

Population and trade contrasted.

Of the articles exported from our own country, nearly the whole of them consists of manufactures of one kind or another, by far the greater part of which consists of textile manufactures, as the following figures will show :—

* See Statistical Abstract for 1870, pages 39 and 75.

C

CHAP. II.

TABLE OF EXPORTS OF TEXTILE MANUFACTURES FOR 1869.*

Cotton manufactures . .	£67,159,064
Woollen ,, . .	28,483,095
Linen ,, . .	9,127,151
Haberdashery, &c. . .	4,582,763
	£109,352,073

Increase in the cotton trade. As was stated in Chapter I., our total export of cotton goods in 1751 amounted only to £45,986. In 1869, notwithstanding the fact that cotton goods are at least five or six times as cheap as they were in 1751, they amount to £67,159,064, or about 1500 times as much in value during the latter period as the former; whilst, if the estimate is taken in bulk, it will amount, at least, to five or six thousand times as much.

The cotton trade in 1869 and 1757 contrasted. For the year (1869) the entire value of our cotton manufactures was upwards of £75,000,000, whereas in 1757, as we have seen, they were only valued at £200,000; or, to put it in another form, though our population has only increased about two and three quarter fold, the yearly value of the cotton goods we produce has increased upwards of 370 fold; and, if we make the calculation by bulk, it will reach about two thousand fold.

Varied application of Machinery. The use of machinery is not however confined to the production of cotton, woollen, and other textile fabrics, it is universally employed in the

---

* See Statistical Abstract for 1870, pages 68 to 75.

manufacture of iron, of paper, in printing, and indeed there is no art or manufacture where labour is employed, which is not very greatly aided by machinery.

The invention of machinery, especially of the steam engine, has contributed very extensively also to develope the mineral resources of our country. If it had not been for the steam engine, a great many of our mines would have been worthless, simply from the fact, that it would have been impossible to pump the water away. *Value of the steam engine.*

MINES.—The following return gives the total weight and value at the pit's mouth of our mineral produce in 1868*:— *Value of our mineral produce*

	TONS.	
Coal	103,141,157	£25,785,289
Pig Iron	4,970,206	12,381,280
Lead	71,017	1,378,404
Other Minerals	22,830	1,976,732
TONS	108,205,210	£41,521,705

In this statement there is no account taken of our stone quarries, limestone rocks, &c. At present there exists, so far as we know, no data by which to estimate them, unless it be by making some valuation of the houses which are constructed from them.

---

* See Statistical Abstract for 1870, page 132. In addition to the minerals given above, there were also 835,512 ounces of Silver, and 1,012 ounces of Gold secured.

CHAP. II.
Number and value of houses in Great Britain.

From the Report of the Commissioners of Inland Revenue for 1870, page 162, we find there are 700,707 houses, each of which pays a yearly rental of over £20, the annual value of the whole being £35,063,843. There are at least 5,000,000 houses under £20; and if we assume that the houses under £20 are of no greater value than those above £20, then, by adding the total rental of house property to the produce of our mines, we get an annual return from the two sources of £111,649,391.

Ultimate value of our mineral produce

As has been stated, however, the estimate which was given of the value of these minerals was their value at the pit's mouth, or about £3. 10s. per ton; but this represents only a portion of what their value becomes ultimately. Most of our mineral produce is used in the construction of machinery, which, when completed, is often sold at £20, £50, and sometimes even £100 or more per ton. If we reckon the average at £20 per ton, it will give a yearly produce from mines alone of upwards of £100,000,000 sterling in value.

RAILWAYS.—The wealth of the United Kingdom invested in, and derivable from, railways, is very large, and is yearly increasing.

Capital invested, in Railways.

It is only about forty years since the first complete railway—the Manchester and Liverpool—was opened; whilst, at the end of 1867, the length of line complete was 14,247 miles; the capital paid up was £502,262,887; number of passengers conveyed, 287,807,904; total receipts, £39,479,999.*

* See Statistical Abstract for 1870, page 131.

The table of imports, which has previously been given, will give a general view of the commerce of the United Kingdom.

In addition to our own commerce, we have also a considerable carrying trade, from which, if we do not get the profit of the trades, we get a considerable income by way of carriage. It may therefore give a more comprehensive and complete view of our commercial progress and position in this respect, if we give a summary of our shipping at the present, as contrasted with bygone times.

The first authoritative return of shipping was issued in 1701-2; at that time the total number of ships in the ports of the United Kingdom was 3,281, which were estimated to carry 261,222 tons, and employed 27,196 men*—the navies of Scotland and Ireland had then scarcely an existence; so that the total for the whole United Kingdom would not be very much in excess of the above. The entire number of vessels belonging to the United Kingdom in 1869 was 21,881, which were estimated to carry 5,557,303 tons, and employed 195,490 men.† The number of vessels which entered our ports in 1869 was 137,652, carrying 18,001,982 tons. The number which left our ports was 138,757, carrying 17,850,749 tons.‡ In the year 1781, the weight of goods which left our ports was only

---

* See McCulloch's Commercial Dictionary, page 1244.

† See Statistical Abstract, for 1870, pages 100 to 104.

‡ See Trade and Navigation Returns for the year ending December, 1869, page 42.

778,994 tons. These figures abundantly illustrate the marvellous development of our commerce during the last 100 or 150 years.

Area of cultivated land.

AGRICULTURE.—The entire area of the United Kingdom, is 77,513,000 acres. Of these, in 1869, 45,880,041 acres, or not much above one-half were under cultivation. The proportion of this area appropriated to different crops is given in the returns as follows* :—

	ACRES.
Wheat	3,981,989
Barley	2,483,277
Oats	4,480,125
Rye	72,986
Beans	584,251
Peas	397,483
	12,000,111
Green and Root Crops, as Potatoes, Turnips, Cabbage, &c.	5,095,933
Other Crops, including 61,729 acres of Hops, also Pasture Land, &c.	29,034,117
Uncultivated and Waste Land	31,382,839
	77,513,000

Uncultivated land.

From the above table it will seen that considerably above one-third of the land of the United

* See Statistical Abstract for 1870, page 111.

Kingdom is still wholly uncultivated; whilst in reference to that which is reported as under cultivation, the produce is so widely various, as to make it absolutely impossible to give any reliable data in respect to our agricultural production.

Yield of land per acre.

Mr. McCulloch, in his "British Empire," estimates the produce of an acre of average good land at thirty-two bushels per acre; the estimate given by the Board of Trade, is twenty-eight bushels per acre.

Backward condition of agriculture.

It is a fact, however, that does not admit of dispute, that whilst for the last hundred years, every other interest in the country has been making the most rapid and marvellous progress, the agricultural interest has nowhere kept pace with the other, and in many districts has scarcely made any progress at all. This partly arises from the ignorance of the farmer, but to a great extent it is owing to the want of security in the tenure of the land. A man who has an uncertain interest in a property, and is not sure but that, if he improves it, others will reap the benefit, can never be expected to improve it as he would if certain to realize the benefit himself.

Mr. Cobden on agriculture.

During the great anti-corn law agitation, the late Mr. Cobden often called attention to the backward state of our agriculture. In one of of his speeches at Manchester,* October 24, 1844, speaking upon this point, and referring to Cheshire, he said: "I have heard Mr. Ogilvy, who was engaged by Mr. Brook, of Mere, and

---

* See his published speeches, vol. 1, page 210.

other landlords of this and the neighbouring county, as superintendent of their estates, declare—and he is willing to go before a Committee of the House of Commons to prove it—that Cheshire, if properly cultivated, is capable of producing three times as much as it now produces from its surface, and he is willing the statement should be made public upon his authority—and there is not a higher authority in the kingdom."

Alderman Mechi, who is one of the greatest of living authorities upon agriculture, asks the question :* " What margin for improvement is there in British agriculture ?" " I have," says he, " tested this by comparative results, and find that, if all the land of this kingdom, 50,000,000 acres, which is equal in quality with my own, produced as much as mine does per acre, our agricultural produce would be increased by the enormous amount of £421,000,000 annually, the present produce, according to my calculation, being only £3. 7s. per acre, or £169,000,000. According to my annual produce of £11. 15s. per acre, it would be £687,000,000." " This," he adds, " is no exaggeration, but a stern and humiliating fact."

This short paragraph reveals to us a twofold fact, viz. :—

1st. The defective condition of our agriculture.

2nd. The vast amount of wealth which our agriculture would yield to us, if only properly attended to.

* Quoted in McDonald's Hints on Farming, page 13.

There is one question, which it will not be out of place to notice here, as it has not only a bearing upon our agriculture and upon our national wealth, but also upon the health and happiness of our cities and towns, and, indeed, of the country generally— I mean the question of sewage. Upon this subject, at the late Social Science Congress, held at Newcastle (September, 1870), a paper was read by Mr. J. T. Blackburn, of Aldershot. The following is the concluding passage of his paper:—

CHAP. II.
On the use of sewage.

"The economic use of sewage is really a national question, bearing very materially upon the food-producing power of the country, not merely from the utilization of the sewage itself, but also indirectly by manure produced by the consumption of so large an addition of green food, where its application to the land becomes general. Milk and butter will be produced at one-third less than their present prices; and it will be found that, when effectually fulfilling the agricultural conditions, it will of necessity accomplish the sanitary object also. Instead of compulsion being needed for its adoption, we shall have active competition.

Mr. J. T. Blackburn on the sewage question.

Alderman Mechi, in a letter to the *Manchester Examiner and Times* of October 20th, 1870, goes more fully into this question. Referring to the farm of Mr. William Hope, at Hornchurch, near Rumford, Essex, he says it receives the whole of the available sewage of that town, containing 8,000 inhabitants. The farm is of 121 acres, of light and poor (generally) soil, which had previ-

Alderman Mechi on the use of sewage.

Mr. Hope's farm.

Mr. Hope's farm continued.

Value of yield per acre.

ously ruined several tenants. He goes on to say: 'Let us compare the condition of this farm now and formerly. Then, three men and two boys were employed; now from 35 to 40 persons are regularly employed, with 16 horses. The crops are enormous and frequent. The minimum value of each crop is £20 per acre; and, as many are perfected in from two to three months, the total value is very considerable."

"While the surrounding farms and market gardens have proved disastrous, owing to the excessive droughts, here the crops have been and are now most abundant and luxuriant, consisting of cauliflowers, cabbages, potatoes, onions, parsnips, carrots, red and Siberian beet, long, red, and globe mangold, and other vegetables, a crop of barley in July, after lettuce is in full ear, Italian rye-grass, already cut five and six times; but the most remarkable is a crop of maize, or Indian corn, eight feet high, as thick in the stem as a mop-stick, with gigantic ears formed and about piercing the sheath. Mr. Hope expects to ripen them, but this I doubt."

"In the meantime, as cattle food, the crop is worth £20 per acre, for horses and cattle are generally fond of it. It seems difficult to realise the fact, that green crops of various kinds should be gathered within ten or twelve weeks after sowing or planting, while those in the neighbourhood are languishing or perishing for want of moisture."

"With sewage, sowing and transplanting become

a certainty in result. Mangolds transplanted in July were a fine crop. I weighed cabbages 20lbs. each, and mangolds would considerably exceed that. .... We thus see, within twelve months, a wretchedly poor farm converted into a most luxuriant garden, its fertility ever increasing, multiplying food and the employment of labour concurrently, and extracting a money value from that which is now, in too many cases, poisoning our streams."

What a revelation is here unfolded! what a source of unapplied wealth does it open out to us! The sewage of our towns and villages, instead of blocking up and poisoning our rivers as it now universally does, might be appropriated to the fertilizing and enriching of the land. By this means—taking Mr. Hope's farm at Hornchurch as a sample—comparatively poor land might rapidly be converted into rich and productive land, yielding annually, not a crop valued at £3. 7s. per acre, but two or three crops yearly, each of them of the value of £20 per acre. Dream of overcrowded population, people starving for want of land upon which to grow food—here is the answer to that bugbear. Let the land only receive in the shape of manure the sewage and refuse from the teeming population of our towns and villages, in addition to the other means which are applied to it, and let it be properly drained and cultivated, and there is hardly any limit to its powers of production.

<small>CHAP. II.
Recuperative power in nature.</small>

There is marvellous wisdom displayed in the arrangements of nature. The earth yields the vegetable produce which supplies food to the animal kingdom. This food, when it has served its purpose in the animal economy, is cast off; but it is not useless waste, for it becomes again available as manure to enrich and fructify the earth—in fact, it is the food of the soil; and in proportion as the soil is thus fed by the sewage and refuse from the animal and vegetable kingdoms, so will be its capability to yield increased food. As the population increases, so will be the demand for food; but in the same proportion there will also be a supply of refuse, or, in other words, of nourishment or manure for the soil. If, therefore, instead of throwing this refuse into our rivers, to block-up and pollute them, we returned it to the land,

<small>*Produce of the soil grows with the population.*</small>

then, as the population increased, there would be an ever-increasing supply of food for the soil, and the yield of produce wherewith to feed the population would increase in the same proportion, and there is no reason (if our resources were properly applied) why the soil of our own country should not easily support a population of over one hundred millions of people.

FISHERIES.—In reference to the fisheries of the United Kingdom, the statistics published are too incomplete to enable us to give anything like a complete and reliable statement.

The number of fishermen engaged are given in the Government returns as follows:— *No. of fishermen employed.*

Isle of Man	2,380
Ireland*	38,444
Scotland†	45,201
Other persons engaged in Scotch fisheries	45,204
	131,229

We may safely assume that there are 20,000 persons engaged in the English fishery trade, and that at least 30,000 other persons are engaged in England, Ireland, and the Isle of Man, in assisting to cure the fish and prepare them for market; if so, it will give us a total of slightly over 180,000 persons who are dependent upon this branch of trade.

In a valuable article on the Fisheries, in the "Encyclopedia Britannica," Sir John Barrow estimates the annual produce of the foreign and domestic fisheries of Great Britain at £8,300,000. This, however, is generally thought to be overstated. McCulloch, in his "Commercial Dictionary," remarks that £5,500,000 will be a full estimate. Whichever of these estimates be correct, one thing is universally admitted, viz., that the fishery trade is capable of very great extension, and if effectually worked would be very prolific in its returns.

Sir John Barrow's estimate of the produce of our fisheries.

McCulloch's estimate.

* See Miscellaneous Statistics, part 7, page 364.
† See Report of Scotch Fisheries issued June 1, 1870, page 22.

In a Report of the Fisheries of the United Kingdom, published in 1866, the Commissioners say:

Produce of the sea.

Report of Royal Commission.

"The produce of the sea around our coasts bears a far higher proportion to that of the land than is generally imagined. The most frequented fishing grounds are much more prolific of food than the same extent of the richest land. Once in the year an acre of good land carefully tilled produces a ton of corn, or two hundredweight or three hundredweight of meat or cheese. The same area at the bottom of the sea, on the best fishing grounds, yields a greater weight of food to the persevering fisherman every week in the year. Five vessels belonging to the same owner, in a single night's fishing, brought in 17 tons weight of fish,—an amount of wholesome food equal to that of 50 cattle, or 300 sheep. The ground which these vessels covered could not have exceeded an area of 50 acres."

The best way to estimate our national resources.

From the facts and figures which have been adduced in this, and the preceding chapter, the reader will be enabled to obtain a tolerably correct idea as to the nature and vast extent of our national resources. The statistics supplied are not, however, sufficiently definite to enable us to give a complete summary of them. In forming an estimate, therefore, as to the total of our national income and resources, much has to be left to conjecture. The most satisfactory approximation to a correct result is, to take the income tax returns as the basis on which to calculate our income.

INCOME OF THE ENTIRE POPULATION OF THE UNITED KINGDOM FOR THE YEAR ENDING MARCH 31, 1870.*

Total income of the United Kingdom.

Schedule (A) In respect of lands, tenements, &c. ...	£133,478,032
„ (B) In respect of the occupation of lands	37,447,774
„ (C) In respect of annuities, dividends, &c.	34,790,120
„ (D) In respect of professions, trades, employments, railways mines, ironworks, &c.	161,594,118
„ (E) In respect of public offices	22,110,858
	£389,420,902
Estimate of incomes under £200, reduced by abatement of £60, and incomes exempt as being under £100, and unreturned profits	120,000,000
Estimated income of the manual labour class	370,000,000
	£879,420,902

The income of the manual labour class is estimated by Professor Leoni Levi at £418,000,000, *Income of the working classes.*

* See Return of Taxes and Imposts moved for by Sir T. Bazley, and ordered to be printed August 10th, 1870.

and by Mr. Dudley Baxter at £325,000,000; if a mean be taken between the two, and we call it say £370,000,000, it will not be far wide of the mark.

It will give the reader an idea as to how much the progress of the wealth of the nation is dependent upon our manufacturing industries, if we give the valuation of property in Lancashire at two periods.

Valuation of property in 1692 and 1865.

Mr. Henry Ashworth, in a paper read at the Friends' Institute, Manchester, gives the real property as assessed for land tax for 1692 and 1865, as follows:—

REAL PROPERTY ASSESSED FOR LAND-TAX IN LANCASHIRE, AT TWO PERIODS.

	Annual Value. 1692	Annual Value. 1865.	Increase of Value.	Rate of Increase.
	£	£	£	
Hundred of Leyland	5,774	249,284	243,510 or	4,317 per Cent
„ Lonsdale	8,500	423,967	415,467 „	4,987 „
„ Amounderness	10,288	526,239	515,951 „	5,115 „
„ Blackburn	11,131	950,916	939,785 „	8,542 „
„ Salford	25,907	4,084,888	4,058,981 „	15,767 „
„ West Derby	35,642	3,801,585	3,765,943 „	10,666 „
	97,242	10,036,879	9,939,637	

Dr. Watts, in his valuable book on the cotton famine, in reference to this table, remarks: "Readers who are acquainted with Lancashire, will not need to be told that the progress is about in proportion to the area occupied for the purposes of manufacture and commerce in each case; that, in fact, the immense stride made by the Salford Hundred (which includes Manchester, &c.) is due to the cotton manufacture, and that of West Derby to the same cause, together with the additional fact, that Liverpool is the grand port of entry for the raw material, and for the departure of manufactured goods."

It may not be uninteresting here to give an estimate of what the nation's income was one hundred years ago. Arthur Young,* in his "Northern Tour," published in the year 1770, estimates the income of England and Wales (not the United Kingdom) as follows :—

Arthur Young's estimate of income in 1770.

INCOME OF ENGLAND AND WALES IN 1770.

Income from the Soil		£66,000,000
,, ,,	Manufactures	27,000,000
,, ,,	Commerce	10,000,000
,, ,,	Law, Physic, the Fine Arts, Literature, &c.	5,000,000
,, ,,	Money Lent at Interest	5,000,000
,, ,,	Public Revenue	9,000,000
		£122,000,000

Arthur Young estimated the population of England and Wales at that time as being 8,500,000; now it is about 22,000,000: so that with a population of rather more than two and

Relative increase of population and income

---

* Quoted in Pictorial History of England, vol. 5, page 582.

On the Sources of

CHAP. II.

a half times what it was one hundred years ago, we have a yearly income of more than six times the income possessed by them.

R. Dudley Baxter's estimate of the property of the United Kingdom

The following is an estimate of the property of the United Kingdom, as given by Mr. R. Dudley Baxter, in his work on the "Taxation of the United Kingdom,"* published 1869.

The property of the United Kingdom is estimated as follows :—

1. REAL PROPERTY—

Lands, houses, and mines were assessed to income tax in 1866, at... £132,000,000

Taken at twenty-three years' purchase, the average number for the total of the three kinds of property, the capitalized value is nearly ... 3,000,000,000

But from this must be deducted the Leaseholds and Mortgages, and Personalty in Mines, estimated at one-third, or............................. 1,000,000,000

Leaving the nett capitalized value of the Real Property of the United Kingdom 2,000,000,000

2. PERSONAL PROPERTY :—

(a) Mortgages, Leaseholds, &c., as above 1,000,000,000

	Annual Value Income Tax, 1865.
(b) Railways, Gas, and Canals ...	£23,000,000
Public Dividends on British, Colonial, and Foreign Funds (Schedule C)	34,000,000
Public Companies	12,000,000
	£69,000,000

Capitalized at twenty-five years' purchase, these amount to 1,700,000,000

---

* See pages 163-164.

		Capital	
(c) Capital estimated to be employed in—			
Farming for £50,000,000 rental, under Schedule A...	£300,000,000	
Trades and Professions for £100,000,000 profit, under Schedule D	500,000,000	
Classes below the Income-tax	200,000,000	
Dead Capital (Furniture, &c.)	300,000,000	
		1,300,000,000
Total Personal Property ...		£4,000,000,000
Total Real and Personal Property, including the National Debt		£6,000,000,000

This is but an insignificant total to be owned by a nation whose yearly income borders on £900,000,000. It proves there is a terrible waste somewhere. We shall see in future chapters where this waste is, and what are its fruits.

It is impossible to take a retrospective view of our resources without being struck with the pre-eminent advantages which in every way we enjoy, and with the mutual fitness of everything to secure the development of our marvellous wealth.

As has been noted in the previous chapter, the situation of our country, its insular position, the suitability of our climate, with other advantages, have all conspired to give us the pre-eminence as a manufacturing and commercial people. The mechanical genius of our countrymen has secured to us the foremost place in regard to machinery, but all this would have been comparatively valueless had it not been for our mineral resources, our iron mines and our coalfields: the one has supplied us with the material with which to construct our machinery, and the other has given us the power by which to put it in motion. These, combined, have placed in our hands such facilities for the acquisition of wealth as has never been enjoyed by any nation in the history of the world. Under such circumstances we should naturally have concluded that our people would universally have been placed far beyond the reach of pauperism and destitution. Alas! this is not the case; for though the wealth of the nation is valued at £6,000,000,000, and its yearly income is estimated at near £900,000,000, still destitution and pauperism deluge us on every hand. How is this?

Having endeavoured as briefly as possible to recapitulate our wealth and its sources, I will now glance at our pauperism, and then try to investigate the cause thereof.

CHAPTER III.

OUR PAUPERISM.

Up to this point, the picture before our eyes has been one of entire brightness. Everything has seemed to be conspiring to pour wealth upon us, and we should naturally expect, that everywhere there would be a universal abundance. Unfortunately, there is a dark side to this picture; for whilst, as a nation, wealth has been pouring upon us, there has been a considerable and a growing proportion of our population sinking in pauperism. Let us briefly glance at this, and then, if we can, in future chapters investigate the causes which reduce so large a proportion of our population to such a deplorable condition. *Condition of our populatio*

The first complete authoritative return that we have as to poor's-rates, is for 1776.* In that year, from returns made upon oath by the overseers of the poor, it appears that the total money raised by assessment for the poor in England and Wales was £1,720,316; last year (1869) it was £11,776,153; or, in other words, with a population rather better than two and a half times the size of what it was one hundred years ago, and with an income six times as large as in 1776, we expended last year *Pauperism now as contrasted with 100 years ago*

---

* See Pictorial History of England, vol. 5, page 582.

nearly seven times as much upon pauperism and crime as we did in 1776. The number of paupers in 1776 is not stated.

The present population of the United Kingdom (1869) is 30,838,210; of these, 1,281,651 are returned as paupers, and 6,692 as vagrants.

The following table will show the gradual and continued increase in our pauperism. It gives the number of paupers in the United Kingdom from 1860 to 1870 inclusive:

Table of paupers for the ten years ending 1870.

	England and Wales.	Scotland.	Ireland.	Total.
1860	851,020	114,209	44,929	1,010,158
1861	890,423	117,113	50,683	1,058,219
1862	946,166	118,928	59,541	1,124,635
1863	1,142,624	120,284	66,228	1,329,136
1864	1,009,289	120,705	68,135	1,198,129
1865	971,433	121,394	69,217	1,162,044
1866	920,344	119,608	65,057	1,105,009
1867	958,824	121,169	68,650	1,148,643
1868	1,034,823	128,976	72,925	1,236,724
1869	1,039,549	128,339	74,745	1,242,633
1870	1,079,391	....	73,921	....

Imperfect character of Government returns as to pauperism, &c.

The Government returns as to pauperism and vagrancy do not, however, by any means represent the extent of these two evils. They give the number of paupers on the books on the 1st day of January, and the number of vagrants who apply for lodging or casual relief on the same day; but this but very imperfectly portrays the pauperism, &c., of the country. According to this method of reckoning, if a man becomes chargeable to the

---

* See Statistical Abstract for 1870, pages 126-7.

union on the 2nd of January, and comes off again on the 31st day of December, he is not counted, though he has been receiving relief during the whole year, except two days. The statistics of the Poor-law Board give the number of paupers and vagrants relieved on one day, (which is what they profess to do), but it does not give the number of persons who get relief as paupers and vagrants during the year. This is the idea generally received, but it is erroneous.

The only complete annual return of paupers issued is for the parochial year 1857. It was furnished by Mr. Purdy, of the Statistical department of the Poor-Law Board, and is given by Mr. Dudley Baxter, in his work on "National Income".*

Return of total No. of paupers during one year.

Paupers, indoor and outdoor, relieved during the half-year ending Michaelmas, 1856 . .	1,845,782
,, ,, only on 1st July, 1856	796,102
Paupers, indoor and outdoor, relieved during the half-year ending Lady Day, 1857 . . .	1,934,286
,, only on 1st January, 1857	843,430
The apparent total for the two half-years is	3,780,068
But from this must be deducted the whole number of paupers relieved on Michaelmas Day, 1856—say	800,000
Leaving the nett total. . .	2,980,000

Being 3½ times the number on the 1st January.

* Page 87.

In order, therefore, to get the number of persons who received relief during 1869, we must multiply 1,281,651 by 3½, which gives 4,485,778. This, then, is the real number of persons who were chargeable as paupers, at one time or another, during that year, or nearly one in seven of the entire population. Admitting that a considerable number of these might be persons who applied twice or three times over during the year, it would still leave us about one in every ten of the population as having been paupers during the course of the year.

In reference to this subject, Mr. Dudley Baxter, in the work just quoted, remarks :—

Mr. Dudley Baxter on pauperism.

"The average number of paupers at one time in receipt of relief in 1866 was 916,000, being less than for any of the four preceding years. The total number relieved during 1866, may, on the authority of a return of 1857, given in the Appendix, be calculated at three and a half times that number, or 3,000,000. All these may be considered as belonging to the 16,000,000 of the manual labour classes, being as nearly as possible twenty per cent on their number; but the actual cases of relief give a very imperfect idea of the loss of work and wages. A large proportion of the poor submit to great hardships, and are many weeks, and even months, out of work before they will apply to the guardians. They exhaust their savings; they try to the utmost their trade unions or benefit societies; they pawn little by little all their furniture; and at last are driven to ask relief."

But even the figures which have been given do not, by any means, represent adequately the pressure of our poverty. There are a very large number of persons who are dependent upon their friends and relations; and there are a number who, as Dudley Baxter says, submit to great hardships sooner than apply for relief. If all who are thus situated be summed up, it cannot amount to much less than one-third of the entire population of the manual labour class, or from fifteen to twenty per cent of the entire population.

Relative No. of paupers to population

The Government returns in reference to vagrancy are even more imperfect and unsatisfactory than the pauper returns. I have not been able to obtain any national figures to illustrate this, but it will be sufficiently manifest if I give the statistics in reference to one union—the Bury Union in which I reside.

The following table gives the number of paupers and vagrants returned to the Poor-law Board, January 1st, 1870, and published in their Report as representing the pauperism and vagrancy in the Bury Union, the population of which, in 1861, was 101,142.

Paupers and vagrants in the Bury Union.

        Paupers 4,372
        Vagrants 11

The actual number of cases of pauperism and vagrancy during the year ending March, 1870, in the Bury Union was as follows:*—

---

* These Returns have been kindly furnished me by W. P. Woodcock, Esq., the clerk to the Bury Union. It will be necessary to deduct from these the 4,372 paupers given above, as the permanent paupers are entered twice during the year. This gives the number of cases of pauperism as 10,640.

CHAP III.

No. of cases of Paupers relieved, 15,012
,, ,, Vagrants ,, 15,474

These returns corroborate the figures given by Mr. Purdy in reference to the pauperism of the country; and they show that if the total cases of vagrancy during the year were given, it wolud numerically be equal to, or greater than the number of paupers.

The same parties often apply several times.

No doubt a very large number of the vagrant cases are from among the paupers, and in a large proportion of the cases, the same parties apply several times over in the same union, and also in different unions; still, it shows that there is a very large class of our population who have no fixed dwelling-place; they move about getting a living by begging, or stealing, or by imposition upon the public, as may be most convenient. Adding this class to the pauper class, it reveals an amount of destitution and demoralisation in the country that is perfectly appalling, and that is a lasting disgrace to our civilization and Christianity. What are the causes of this condition of things? and what are the remedies to be applied? To give an answer to these questions will be the object of the succeeding chapters in this book.

CHAPTER IV.

ON THE FALLING OFF IN TRADE.

During the four years subsequent to the recent American civil war, the trade of this country, especially the cotton trade, was in a most precarious and unprofitable condition; so continuously and ruinously bad was it, that a very general belief became prevalent in commercial circles, that the manufacturing industries of this country had had their day, and that they were about to pass into the hands of other nations. It was commonly said on the Manchester Exchange, that there had been so many mills erected on the continent, as enabled them not only to supply their own wants, but to create a surplus for disposal elsewhere; and it was said that, what with lower wages and longer hours, our continental neighbours were outstripping us, and beating us, not only in their own and in neutral markets, but actually in the markets of London and Manchester, and that, by and bye, much of our trade would be a thing of the past.

Being largely interested in the cotton trade, as a spinner and manufacturer, the writer shared in the general fear and despondency. It appeared to him that if the cotton trade was about to pass

Depressed condition of trade after the close of the American War.

Foreign competition the supposed cause

The Author investigates the question.

CHAP. IV.

away—if the ship was about to sink—the sooner he got out of her and the better. As a prudent man, however, he thought it would only be wise before taking such an important step to ascertain whether this was really the fact or not; whether our bad trade arose from a falling off in the foreign demand, or it arose from a diminution in the home trade.

The depression caused by the falling off in the Home trade.

An examination of the question established the fact that there had been no falling off in our foreign trade, but a considerable increase; and that this was the case not only in reference to the general export trade, but even to our trade with those continental countries which were said to be outstripping us, but that, whilst our foreign trade had continued to grow, our home trade in cotton goods had fallen off to a considerable extent, and that this falling off had not been made up for by an equivalent increase in the woollen and linen trades.

Comparison of trade with ten years ago.

The four years ending 1861 (which were prior to the American war), were the four most prosperous years which the cotton trade, or indeed the general trade of this country, ever experienced. The prevailing impression has been that the year 1860 was the turning point, and that from that time our trade has been retrograding. Is this so? In order to test it, I will give a comparison of our foreign, and also, as far as possible, of our home trade in cotton, woollen, and linen, for the four years ending 1861, and the four years ending 1869.

On the Falling Off in Trade. 45

TABLE OF EXPORTS OF COTTON, WOOLLEN, AND LINEN GOODS, FOR THE FOUR YEARS ENDING 1861, AND THE FOUR YEARS ENDING 1869.*

QUANTITY OF COTTON GOODS EXPORTED.

Cotton Goods—Yards.		Cotton Goods—Yards.	
1858	2,324,139,085	1866	2,575,698,138
1859	2,562,545,476	1867	2,832,023,707
1860	2,776,218,427	1868	2,977,106,551
1861	2,563,459,007	1869	2,866,113,363
	10,226,361,995		11,250,941,759

Quantity of cotton goods exported.

Being an increase in the quantity of our exports during the latter period, as compared with the former, of 1,024,579,764 yards, or 10 per cent.

VALUE† OF COTTON GOODS EXPORTED.

Cotton Goods—Value.‡		Cotton Goods—Value.	
1858	£43,001,322	1866	£74,613,046
1859	48,202,225	1867	70,836,983
1860	52,012,380	1868	67,686,772
1861	46,872,489	1869	67,159,064
	£190,088,416		£280,295,865

Value of cotton goods exported.

Or an increase in the value of cotton goods exported of £90,207,449, or 47 per cent.

QUANTITY OF WOOLLEN GOODS EXPORTED.

Woollen Goods—Yards.		Woollen Goods—Yards.	
1858	166,141,745	1866	281,878,523
1859	193,687,679	1867	249,459,211
1860	190,371,537	1868	269,134,508
1861	164,398,181	1869	303,016,569
	714,599,142		1,103,488,811

Quantity of woollen goods exported.

* See Statistical Abstract for 1870, pages 64-65. The particulars for cotton, woollen, and linen will all be found in the same table.

† The values represent both cloth and yarns; the quantities represent cloth only.

‡ See Statistical Abstract for 1870, pages 68-69. The particulars for cotton, woollen, and linen will all be found in the same table.

Being an increase in our export of woollen goods during the four years ending 1869 of 388,889,669 yards, or 54 per cent.

VALUE OF WOOLLEN GOODS EXPORTED.

Woollen Goods—Value.		Woollen Goods—Value.	
1858	£12,743,867	1866	£26,538,379
1859	15,137,769	1867	25,943,928
1860	16,000,448	1868	25,900,084
1861	14,671,668	1869	28,483,095
	£58,553,752		£106,865,486

Showing an increase in the value of woollen goods exported of £48,311,734, or 83 per cent.

QUANTITY OF LINEN GOODS EXPORTED.

Linen Goods—Yards.		Linen Goods—Yards.	
1858	121,940,291	1866	255,468,689
1859	138,120,498	1867	211,275,196
1860	143,996,773	1868	210,049,678
1861	116,322,469	1869	214,715,319
	520,380,031		891,508,882

Being an increase in the quantity of linen goods exported of 361,128,851 yards, or 71 per cent.

VALUE OF LINEN GOODS EXPORTED.

Linen Goods—Value.		Linen Goods—Value.	
1858	£5,870,696	1866	£11,950,377
1859	6,279,189	1867	9,887,776
1860	6,606,075	1868	9,422,367
1861	5,474,557	1869	9,127,151
	£24,230,517		£40,387,671

Showing an increase in the value of linen goods exported of £16,157,154, or 67 per cent.

From the preceding tables it will be manifest that the increase in the value of cotton goods exported for the four years ending 1869, over the four years ending 1861, was 47 per cent; of woollen goods, 83 per cent.; and of linen goods, 67 per cent, making an average increase in the value of our exports in ten years of 66 per cent, the greatest increase which ever occurred in the same time, and a very different thing from the falling off that was commonly believed to have been the case.

Chap. IV.
Relative increase of exports.

If the value of goods recede to the level of the prices they were at before the American war, so that the enormous increase in the value of our exports shall represent a corresponding increase in their bulk; and if, as it is only natural to expect, the high prices which have been prevalent in goods has led to their use being minimized as much as possible, the world must generally be bare of goods, and therefore, it becomes almost a certainty that our foreign trade, more particularly in cotton goods, must very much increase. If we get a cheap and abundant supply of cotton, as appears likely ere long, there is a bright prospect before the cotton trade, especially if there should be a revival in the home trade.

Deduction from the foregoing figures.

In the home trade there are not the same statistical returns published as in the export trade; nevertheless our home consumption of cotton goods may be calculated with sufficient nicety to be reliable. To come at this, we have the amount of cotton imported, and then the amount taken by the

Home trade returns.

trade; then we have the published tables of exports of goods, and deducting the exports from the total cotton used, it will give us the home consumption.

Mr. Elijah Helm's calculation as to the Home trade.

Mr. Elijah Helm, in a paper read before the Manchester Statistical Society, and which has been published and largely circulated amongst the leading manufacturers and merchants in Lancashire, has gone into these calculations elaborately.

He has kindly given me a copy of his paper, from which I extract the following tables of quantities; the tables of values I have added, calculating them on the same basis as the exports.

ESTIMATED WEIGHT OF COTTON CONTAINED IN MANUFACTURES OF ALL KINDS EXPORTED AND RETAINED FOR HOME CONSUMPTION.

Total weight of cleaned cotton used.

1858 815,040,000	1866 824,130,000
1859 878,940,000	1867 859,680,000
1860 975,240,000	1868 886,860,000
1861 906,660,000	1869 847,362,000
3,575,880,000	3,418,032,000

Showing a reduction in the total of cotton used during the last four years, as compared with the former, of 157,848,000 lbs., or rather over 4 per cent.

WEIGHT OF CLEANED COTTON IN YARN AND MANUFACTURES EXPORTED.

Weight used in goods and yarns exported.

1858 670,034,000	1866 664,093,000
1859 710,310,000	1867 747,256,000
1860 757,267,000	1868 779,397,000
1861 701,406,000	1869 752,091,000
2,839,017,000	2,942,837,000

Being an increase in the quantity of cotton used in goods for exportation of 103,820,000lbs., or rather more than 3½ per cent.

For the sake of comparison I here repeat the table of the value of our export of cotton goods.

VALUE OF COTTON GOODS OF ALL KINDS EXPORTED.

1858	..	£43,001,322	1866 ...	£74,613,046
1859	...	48,202,225	1867 ...	70,836,983
1860	...	52,012,380	1868 ...	67,686,772
1861	...	46,872,489	1869 ..	67,159,064
		£190,088,416		£280,295,865

Value of cotton goods exported.

Or an increase in the value of goods exported of £90,207,449, or 47 per cent.

WEIGHT OF CLEANED COTTON IN MANUFACTURES RETAINED FOR HOME CONSUMPTION.

1858	145,006,000	1866	160,037,000
1859	168,630,000	1867	112,424,000
1860	217,973,000	1868	107,463,000
1861	205,254,000	1869	95,271,000
	736,863,000		475,195,000

Weight of cleaned cotton in goods for Home consumption.

Being a decrease in the cotton used for goods for home consumption of 261,668,000lbs., or more than 35 per cent.

VALUE OF COTTON GOODS OF ALL KINDS, RETAINED FOR HOME CONSUMPTION.

1858	...	£9,306,169.	1866 ...	£17,980,686
1859	...	11,443,371	1867 ...	10,657,361
1860	...	14,971,330	1868 ...	9,332,629
1861	...	13,716,400	1869 ...	8,501,737
		£49,437,270		£46,472,413

Value of cotton goods used in the Home trade.

D

The fall off in cotton not substituted.

Showing a decrease also in the value of cotton goods for home consumption of £2,959,231, or 6 per cent.

It has generally been alleged, as a reason for the falling off in the home trade in cotton goods, that it has arisen from the fact that woollen and linen have been to a very large extent, substituted. It has been said, there has been a falling off in cotton goods, but there has not been a falling off in trade generally: what has been lost in cotton has been gained in woollen and linen. Is this so? In the annual Trade Review of Messrs. Ellison and Haywood, Brokers, Liverpool, for the year 1869, I find the following comparison of the linen and woollen trade for the four years ending 1861 with the four years ending 1869:

TOTAL CONSUMPTION OF WOOLLEN AND LINEN, BOTH FOR THE HOME AND EXPORT TRADE.

Relative increase in woollen and linen.

	1858-61. lbs.	1866-69. lbs.	Increase.	Increase per cent.
TOTAL CONSUMPTION.				
Woollen...	179,698,000	241,070,000	61,372,000	34
Linen ...	169,256,000	232,131,000	62,875,000	37
TOTAL EXPORT.				
Woollen...	106,691,000	162,498,000	55,807,000	52
Linen ...	84,590,000	125,283,000	40,693,000	48
TOTAL HOME CONSUMPTION.				
Woollen...	73,007,000	78,572,000	5,565,000	7·2
Linen ...	84,666,000	106,848,000	22,182,000	26

Great falling off in Home consumption.

From the tables which have been given, it will be manifest that, whilst the weight of cotton used in goods for home consumption has decreased 261,668,000 lbs. during the four years ending 1869, as compared with the four years ending 1861, the total increase both of woollen and linen (notwithstanding the increase in population) has only amounted to 27,747,000 lbs., or not much above a tenth part of the falling off in cotton.

From a consideration of the statistics which have been given, we may logically draw the following conclusion :

> 1st. That the belief which was prevalent a short time ago, that our trade is being supplanted by Continental manufacturers, is all a delusion, inasmuch as our exports of manufactured goods have enormously increased ; whilst our home consumption has very considerably fallen off.
>
> 2nd. That the main, if not the only, cause of the great depression which has latterly existed in our trade, especially in the cotton trade, has arisen from this falling off in the home trade.

What are the causes which have induced this falling off?

There are a variety of opinions upon this subject. Some have said that it has been caused by the poverty of the people; others have ascribed it to the panic of 1866; others have said that Trades Unions have had much to do with it ; whilst others allege that it has arisen from over-speculalation. Doubtless, all these and other things have had an influence; but the combined influence of all has been insignificant as compared to the influence arising from the intemperate habits of the people.

This question is one of vast importance; I therefore ask the reader's careful attention whilst I dwell upon it. Before, however, I enter upon its discussion, I propose to devote a chapter to the consideration of the question of Productive and Non-productive Labour and Expenditure.

CHAPTER V.

PRODUCTIVE AND NON-PRODUCTIVE LABOUR AND EXPENDITURE.

WEALTH is generally defined to be, "That which has an exchange value;" or in other words, anything that can be sold or that will fetch a price in the world's market may be called wealth, the value of such wealth depending upon the cost of its production, which cost is determined by the amount of labour that is expended upon it.

Adam Smith[*] says: "The annual labour of any nation is the fund which originally supplies it with all the necessaries and conveniences of life which it annually consumes, and which consists always in the immediate produce of that labour, or with what is purchased with that produce from other nations.

"According, therefore, as this produce, or what is purchased with it, bears a greater or smaller proportion to the number of those who consume it, the nation will be better or worse supplied with all the necessaries and conveniences for which it has occasion.

"But this proportion must in every nation be

[*] See Wealth of Nations, page 1.

regulated by two different circumstances, first, by the skill, dexterity, and judgment with which its labour is generally applied; and secondly, by the proportion of those who are employed in useful labour, and of those who are not so employed.

"Whatever be the soil, climate, or extent of territory of any particular nation, the abundance or scantiness of its annual supply must in that particular situation depend upon those two circumstances."

Sir W. G. Armstrong on labour as the source of value.

At the Social Science Congress, held at Newcastle, September, 1870, Sir W. G. Armstrong read a paper on economy and trade, in which he puts the matter in the following words :—

"Labour, physical and mental, is the creative element of our nation; nothing possesses value until labour has been expended upon it; not even raw material is exempted from this rule. Gold itself is entirely valueless as it is mixed with the sands of rivers. It is only by labour expended upon its collection that it acquires value, and its dearness is only an expression of the great amount of that labour. Analyze it as we will, we always come to labour as the foundation of value."

What determines the gain of wealth.

These are truths which are now so generally recognised by political economists, that it is unnecessary further to dwell upon them. The point to which I wish specially to direct the reader's attention is this, that the difference between what is created by the labour of a nation, or of an individual, and what is destroyed by them, whether by consumption or waste, is the measure of their gain or loss in wealth.

Adam Smith,* referring to this point, says: "Both productive and unproductive labourers, and those who do not labour at all, are all equally maintained by the lands and labour of the country. This produce, how great so ever, can never be infinite; but must have certain limits. According, therefore, as a greater or smaller proportion of it is in any one year employed in maintaining unproductive hands, the more in the one case, and the less in the other, will remain for the productive, and the next year's produce will be greater or smaller accordingly; the whole annual produce, if we except the spontaneous productions of the earth, being the effect of productive labour."

Adam Smith on productive and unproductive labour.

When labour is rightly applied, and reasonable economy is practised, the accumulative power of human industry is something marvellous.

The rapidly accumulating power of industry.

If we take agriculture, in which there has probably been the least improvement, and where, up to the present time, machinery has been less applied than in any other department of labour, one man will cultivate sufficient land to produce food for the support of at least twenty persons.

In Agriculture.

In the manufacture of clothing, owing to the extensive application of machinery, there is a much greater productive power. If we take the pro-

In manufacturing.

---

* See Wealth of Nations, Book II., chap. 3.

duction of cotton goods as an example, I find that a cotton mill containing 800 looms, and employing 667 hands (most of whom are females, and many of them children from nine to fifteen years of age), will produce more than 7,000,000 yards of calico per annum. The average consumption of calico during the year 1868-9 by the people of this country was not more than 18 yards per head, so that dividing the quantity produced among the workers, we find that one person will produce as much cotton cloth as will supply at least 550 people. These remarks apply with equal force to the manufacture of other articles of clothing, so that, taking the whole of what man needs in the shape of clothing, it may be safely asserted that one person will produce as much as will supply at least 50 people.

In Building. In addition to food and clothing, there only remains to be provided, houses to dwell in, and furniture to stock the houses with. After carefully investigating this matter, I feel safe in assuming that to supply these, would, at the outside, require no more labour than is necessary in providing our supply of food: if so, then the total amount of labour needed to provide for our wants will be as follows; Food, half an hour's labour daily; clothing, fifteen minutes' labour daily; houses, &c., half-an-*Amount of daily toil needed to supply man's wants.* hour's labour, that is, (assuming every person did their share), a total of $1\frac{1}{4}$ hour's daily labour would suffice to supply us in abundance with all the comforts of life. The progress of invention, and the increasing application of machinery, are daily reducing even this amount of labour, so that the part which has now mainly to be played by man is, simply to superintend the machinery which does the work.

End of man's existence.

I know I shall be here reminded that people are not contented merely with the comforts of life, but that they seek also to enjoy themselves; hence, much of the nation's income is expended upon mere luxuries, and, as a consequence, a great portion of the labour which is needed, is needed simply to supply the waste either of luxury or intemperance. If man were only to act as becomes the dignity of his character, and seek enjoyment in cultivating the higher faculties of his nature, instead of that which is merely sensual, it would vastly enhance human happiness, and reduce our enormous wasteful expenditure, which involves so much of time to replace it; and it would bring him more in unison with the position his Maker intended that he should occupy.

Human happiness not in sensuality.

Political economists generally divide labour into two classes, viz., productive and non-productive.

Two classes of labour.

Productive labour is that kind of labour which adds directly to the utility, or in other words, which increases the value, or supposed value, of a thing, thereby increasing the sum of wealth; such is the labour of the farmer, the mechanic, the stonemason, and indeed of artizans and mill operatives generally.

Productive labour.

By non-productive labour is generally understood, the labour of such persons as are not directly

Non-productive labour.

engaged in the production of wealth—to wit, soldiers, policemen, physicians, agents, schoolmasters, and others.

These definitions not strictly accurate.

It will however be obvious, that whilst in a general sense this classification may be considered correct, yet if it be examined minutely it will be seen to be misleading. The energies of the physician or the schoolmaster, for instance, may not, like the stonemason or the mechanic, be employed in the direct production of material wealth; but surely those whose labours are directed to the improvement of the human race are more productively

Occupation of the Mechanic.

employed than they would be if engaged in dressing a stone or improving a piece of iron; their labour is of the highest, and, in the long run, of the most productive kind, whether materially or morally.

The occupation of the policeman, soldier, &c., however, is very different. Their labour adds directly no value to anything. If they are of

Occupation of the Soldier, &c.

value in any sense, it can only be in that of giving greater security to the rights and property of the community. The necessity for this protection, however, arises from the disordered condition of society. Under such circumstances all rational effort will be best directed when applied not merely to providing this physical-force protection, but to removing the causes which lie at the root of the

These occupations necessary, owing to our imperfect state.

disorders which prevail. By such application the need for merely protective service will be diminished, which might then be employed in labour more directly productive.

Strictly speaking, a non-producer is a person who consumes or destroys an amount equivalent to what he produces, so that at the end of the year, or at the termination of life, the world is no better off (materially) for his having been in it; in one sense he is a producer, but as he consumes or destroys more than he produces, he does nothing to increase the general wealth.

Political economists generally speak only of producers or non-producers, but there is a large class of the community that belongs to neither.

Let me illustrate what I mean:—

If a man earns twenty shillings weekly, and only consumes twelve shillings out of the twenty for his support, or for other purposes, then he produces eight shillings weekly more than he consumes—he is in the fullest sense a producer. If, however, he earns twenty shillings, and uses the whole twenty, then he really produces nothing, because at the end of the year he will have consumed or destroyed as much as he has produced. He is therefore a non-producer. But if the man earns only twenty shillings, and consumes or wastes twenty-five, then the world loses five shillings weekly by his existence. To style such an one a non-producer is only to tell part of the truth, because he destroys five shillings per week more than he gets. Such a man can therefore only be correctly described as a destroyer.

There is a very common but erroneous popular belief, that destruction of property is good for

Chap. v.

True definition of a producer.

Illustrations of productive and non-productive labour.

60   *Productive and Non-productive*

CHAP. V.
To destroy property does not increase the demand for labour.

trade, inasmuch as it is thought to create a demand for material, to replace that which has been destroyed. I can best show the fallacy of this notion by giving an illustration. I will assume that a certain person, A, is worth his £50,000; of this he has £20,000 invested in a mill. The rest of his money he has partly in the bank, and partly in sundry other investments. He however finds that the £20,000 he has invested in the mill pays him the best interest, and therefore he is contemplating doubling the size of his mill, so as to find employment for another £20,000. Whilst revolving these schemes in his mind, a fire occurs, and his mill is burnt to the ground. People say, "It's a bad job, but it's good for trade." Is this so? Those who talk thus should not forget that the money which will re-build the burnt mill, would have built a second mill. In that case there would have been two mills instead of one; and instead of 250 workpeople being needed, there would have been 500;

It diminishes it.

there would have been a double demand for labour, and a double production of goods; or, in other words, a double creation of wealth.

Productive investment in case of bad trade.

It might, however, possibly be the case that trade was bad, and that owing to food being dear, and there being no demand for manufactured goods, A. could hardly sell the produce of his first mill. Under such circumstances, therefore, he would not think of building a second. In that case—What should he do? Burn his mill down in order that he might find use for his money? No;

but look out for some other investment. Very likely he might see it most profitable to invest his £20,000 in an estate, and set men to work to drain and improve it, so as to secure better and larger crops. By so doing, he would find additional labour for the workmen, increase the supply of food, and thereby reduce its price; and so, by lowering the cost of food, he would secure increased means by which to purchase manufactured goods, and they augment the general trade and commerce of the country.

In considering these matters, people overlook the fact that the wealth of a nation is the wages fund out of which employment is found for labour. It is the desire of those who have money to use it; and it can only be profitably used by being employed in some kind of labour. If a man has but £20,000, he will be able to employ only half the labour that he would if he had £40,000. If, therefore, the wealth of a community, or of an individual, be diminished, the power to employ labour will be diminished in the same proportion.

The nation's wealth is its wages fund.

If wealth be diminished the demand for labour is diminished in proportion.

In considering the question of labour, it should not be lost sight of that the kind of labour in which persons are employed is a point of vital importance.

Rightly directed labour important.

There are two ways in which an error may be committed in this respect, viz.:—

1st. By labour being employed upon objects of a hurtful or questionable nature.

2nd. By its being employed to purposes that yield no return.*

Example of unproductive labour.

Suppose that I employ fifty men at 15s. per week, and that on the Monday morning I set them to work to dig a large hole; I keep them so employed till Saturday morning, when I order them to fill the hole up again; I pay them £37. 10s. for the week's work, or after the rate of £1,800 per annum. What have they done? They have been kept at work all the week, but on the Saturday night, things are exactly as they were on the Monday morning. There has been nothing produced.

Erroneous ideas respecting labour.

But then it is said, though nothing has been produced, it has been a good job for the men. They have had a week's work, and the world, if it is not richer, is none the poorer. Is it not? What then has become of the food which the men have eaten? of the clothing and other material they have worn during the week? If the men have spent all their wages to maintain themselves during the week of unproductive labour, then it follows that the world is £37. 10s. poorer at the end of the

---

* Professor Fawcett has some very pertinent observations on this point. His remarks are:—

First.—A man may spend money on luxuries; then capital is consumed in simply giving him pleasure.

Second.—A man may spend capital on unproductive labour; then capital is consumed in simply giving food to the labourers.

Third.—A man may spend capital on productive labour; then capital is not only reproduced, but also gives the same amount of support to the labourers as in the second case.

See Manual of Political Economy, page 25.

week than at the beginning. This is indisputable, because, the men have consumed that amount of value during the week, and have produced nothing in its place.

If, however, during the week the fifty men had been employed in digging half a score of cottage cellars, then there would have been something to show, as a set-off against what they had consumed. The world would have been poorer by the food, &c., but it would have been richer by the cellars, which would be a permanent addition to the value, comfort, and utility of the ten cottages.

It may be said that the case here supposed is an extreme one, and one that never occurs, because nobody would be so foolish as to spend his money upon what would realize no return.

I admit that the case appears an extreme one as compared with the others; but it only seems extreme because it is put in a way that is not usually acted upon. Men do not usually lay out their money in employing men to dig holes and fill them up again, but they do often spend money in ways which are not a whit more productive, and very much more pernicious.

Let me illustrate this, by giving two or three cases.

It is commonly believed that a wealthy, fast-going, spendthrift sort of fellow, who may perchance come to live in some country village, and who spends his money extravagantly in luxurious living, is a good friend to trade. "See!" it is said,

Example of productive labour.

Erroneous ideas as to expenditure.

"what money he pours into the village." Let us examine this position a little more closely.

<small>CHAP. V.</small>

<small>Case supposed.</small>

Let it be granted that the individual referred to spends—say £1,800 a year. Does he by his expenditure in anywise add to the wealth of the community? It is true that he puts £1,800 a year into the tills of the shopkeepers, publicans, or other tradesmen in the locality; but then, if he does this, he abstracts £1,800 worth of goods from their shelves or their cellars. What become of these? He and his dependents consume or waste them. At the end of the year the shopkeepers have got his money, but they have parted with their goods, and beyond the trifling profit which the shopkeepers may have made upon the transaction, they are no richer than at the beginning of the year, whilst the spendthrift himself is £1,800 poorer, for he has parted with his money, and has nothing to show in its place.

<small>Luxurious living.</small>

<small>Prodigal expenditure results in waste.</small>

It may be said, that such a fellow goes in for enjoyment, and that in this way he receives a *quid pro quo* for the money he spends. My business here is not to argue this point, but to show the influence of such conduct in its relation to our national wealth. It may not, however, be improper to remind the reader that such enjoyments are mainly sensual; they neither improve nor increase the happiness of mankind, but rather tend to their demoralization, and consequently to the diminution of their happiness. Human actions, when in accordance with Divine law, invariably tend to advance-

<small>Human enjoyment in harmony with progressive wealth.</small>

ment, whether in material, mental, or moral wealth; and unless in what we do this result be attained, we may seriously ask ourselves the question whether we are in the right track, or not.

Let us suppose that the individual to whom we have referred, instead of wasting £1,800 in luxurious and extravagant living, had invested it in the erection of—say, a dozen good cottages. In this case, he would have found a year's employment for at least a score of men. These men would have been kept industriously employed; they would have received the money as wages, and paid it to the shopkeeper for goods, and at the end of the year the village would be blessed with a dozen good houses, augmenting the wealth and increasing the comfort of the people for generations to come.

In one case there is £1,800 spent, which goes into the pockets of the shopkeepers, &c., but there is nothing to show in place of it; the £1,800 is wasted, and, in addition to the waste, there has been a vicious example set in the prodigal's extravagance. In the other case, the £1,800 gives a year's employment to twenty workmen, thereby giving encouragement to habits of industry; and at the end of the year there are a dozen good houses, which add to the wealth and greatly increase the happiness and comfort of the people; the shopkeepers get the benefit in this case equally as much as in the other case, only, the money is

E

Adam Smith on prodigal expenditure.

paid to them through the twenty industrious workmen, instead of direct from the prodigal owner of the £1,800.

Adam Smith,* referring to prodigal expenditure, says : " The prodigal, by not confining his expense within his income, encroaches upon his capital ; he pays the wages of idleness with those funds which the frugality of his forefathers had, as it were, consecrated to the maintenance of industry. By diminishing the funds destined for the employment of productive labour, he necessarily diminishes, so far as it depends upon him, the quantity of that labour, which adds a value to the subject upon which it is bestowed, and consequently the value of the annual produce of the land and labour of the whole country, the net wealth and revenue of its inhabitants."

" If the prodigality of some were not compensated by the frugality of others, the conduct of every prodigal, by feeding the idle with the bread of the industrious, would tend not only to beggar himself but to impoverish the country."

Prodigal expenditure the same—whether in home or foreign trade.

" This expense, it may be said, indeed, not being in foreign goods, and not occasioning any exportation of gold and silver, the same quantity of money would remain in the country as before. But if the quantity of food and clothing which were thus consumed, by unproductive, had been distributed among productive hands, they would have re-produced, together with a profit, the full

* See Wealth of Nations, Book II., chap. 3.

value of consumption. The same quantity of money would in this case equally have remained in the country, and there would besides, have been a reproduction of an equal value of consumable goods: there would have been two values instead of one."

It may not be the case, perhaps, that in every village there is such an extravagant spendthrift as the one I have described, but if there be not one individual who of himself squanders £1,800 a year, there are a great many individuals who squander five, ten, twenty, or, perhaps, eighty or one hundred pounds yearly. In these cases the result amounts in the aggregate to the same thing as in the individual case referred to.

But the £1,800 is often spent even in a still worse way.

There are very few villages which have not their three or four public-houses or beershops. At the very lowest computation, where four of these exist they involve an expenditure on the part of the population of at least £1,800. At the end of the year, what is there to show for this? There is nothing; unless it be misery, want, and vice. The £1,800 has been spent, but there is no return. It is lost; nay, worse than lost; for the manufacture of every pound's worth of intoxicating liquor involves a destruction of grain equal to eight 4lb. loaves, and therefore the manufacture of £1,800 worth of intoxicating liquors will involve the destruction of grain equal to 14,400 loaves. It is

Chap. v.

An aggregate of small cases equivalent to one large one.

£1,800 spent in intoxicating drink.

No return but misery.

Grain destroyed thereby.

as if the man who dug the large hole at an expense of £1,800, in filling it up again had buried 14,400 loaves in it. Nay! the spending of money in drink involves consequences even worse than these; for there is in addition to these two losses, the creation of disease, vice, and innumerable social and moral evils. It would be well if the money spent on drink were paid to men to dig holes and fill them up again, for then the loss of the money would be the whole of the evil. Nay, more, it would be well if, in addition to the spending of £1,800 upon the hole, there were only 14,400 loaves buried in it, for then the loss of the money and the loaves would be the sum of the evil; but when the money is expended upon drink, this is not all. There is first, loss of money; second, destruction of grain; and then last, but not least, there is the ruin of the people's virtues, the loss of social and domestic comfort, and other evils which degrade the community and sadden the heart. If the money were paid to get rid of these evils, it would be an expenditure worthy of rational beings; but to buy them, and at such a price, too, would be deemed insanity, if it were not manifest before our eyes.

There are some, who upon many questions are very intelligent people, who hold the notion that so long as money does not go out of the country, it matters not in what way it is spent; for, say they, the money is still in existence; it is not destroyed, but simply transferred from one pocket to another.

These persons argue as though money alone was wealth, whereas, strictly speaking, it is only the representative of wealth; and they overlook the fact, too, that when there is a transfer of money from the buyer's to the seller's pocket, there should be a transfer of some equivalent from the seller to the buyer; or, as Adam Smith puts it—there should be not one value only, but two.

Let me illustrate this point by a comparison of two cases.

I will first of all suppose the case of a man who, at the end of the week, goes to the public-house, and spends, say, ten or fifteen shillings upon intoxicating liquors. On the Monday morning he goes to his work, minus his money; and what has he got to show in its place? Nothing; unless, which is very probable, he may have got a severe headache, to be rid of which he would possibly be glad to pay another half-crown. Except this headache, however, he has nothing.*

But then, says our objector, if the man has not

---

* It may, perhaps, be objected to the argument here used, that it owes its existence and force entirely to the man's folly; that if, when the man spent the fifteen shillings on the beer or spirits, instead of consuming it all in one or two days or in a week, and thus degrading himself to drunkenness, he had taken a gill or a pint daily, and extended its use over a period of two or three months, that then such use would be legitimate, and the argument would be inapplicable. If I admitted the validity of this reasoning, it in no way affects the question, because, unfortunately, the argument is founded upon things as they are. Reduce the evil, and the force of the argument is reduced correspondingly. If the ideal of the gill per day could be realised, the question would then perhaps fall more within the domain of the total abstainer, than of the political economist.

the money, the publican has got it; the money is not lost, and so far as the general public is concerned it makes no matter; the cash has simply changed hands.

Fifteen shillings spent on a pair of shoes.

It may best expose the absurdity of this, if we look at the other case. On the Saturday evening the other man goes and spends ten or fifteen shillings likewise. How does he spend it? Perhaps in buying a pair of shoes. In the first case, the publican has got the ten or fifteen shillings, but the man who spent it with him has nothing. In the latter case, the shoemaker (like the publican) gets the ten or fifteen shillings, and his customer gets a pair of shoes. To put the contrast plainly, it is—

A contrast.

Publican, ten or fifteen shillings. Customer, nothing (except headache).

Shoemaker, ten or fifteen shillings. Customer, pair of good shoes.

In the words of Adam Smith, in the latter case there are two values instead of one.

Fifteen shillings spent on food.

I might have supposed that, instead of purchasing a pair of shoes, the man had spent his ten or fifteen shillings in the purchase of food. In that case—What would have been the result? The food purchased would, of course, have been consumed, as in the case of the beer; but during its consumption it would have supplied the man with nourishment for a couple of weeks, during which time he would reproduce by his labour an equivalent, or more than an equivalent, for that which he consumes. If he

Labour and Expenditure. 71

were engaged in calico weaving, he would, during the fortnight, produce 1,000 yards of calico; there would then have been

Fifteen shillings worth of food consumed,—but
One thousand yards of calico produced.

The world would have been poorer by the food used, but richer by the calico produced.

Let us take an illustration upon a more extended scale from the county of Lancashire.

In this county, according to the census of 1861, there is a population of 2,429,440; its area is 1,219,221 acres; the number of public-houses is 7,844; beerhouses 9,889; making a total of 17,733 places (exclusive of wine shops, &c.) where intoxicating liquors are sold. The total number of public-houses and beershops in the United Kingdom in 1869 was 150,599; the amount expended on drink in 1869 was £112,885,603, which would give as spent at each house an average of £750. If we multiply the 17,733 public-houses and beerhouses in Lancashire by this figure, it will give an expenditure for the county of Lancashire in intoxicating drinks during 1869 of £13,299,750. Our inquiry is—
1st. What are the results of this expenditure? and 2nd. What results would accrue if the money were spent as it ought to be?

First. What results to Lancashire from the expenditure on intoxicating liquors in 1869? Let the reader seriously ponder the catalogue :—

1. £13,299,750 directly spent upon intoxicating liquors.

Chap. v.

Expenditure upon intoxicating drinks in Lancashire.

What results from the drink expenditure.

2. £1,113,244 paid in Poor and Police Rates.
3. 102,694 paupers.
4. 30,000 (or more) vagrants idling as vagabonds about the streets.
5. 4,706 lunatics.
6. 3,749 inquests.
7. 90,257 persons brought before the magistrates and convicted of crime.
8. 5,913 depredators, offenders, and suspected persons who are abroad.
9. 2,749 houses of bad character, brothels, receivers of stolen goods, &c.
10. 3,316 policemen employed to protect society from the dangers arising therefrom.
11. 17,733 public-houses and beershops.
12. 70,932 drunkards, filling innumerable homes with misery.
13. 7,000,000 or more bushels of grain destroyed in manufacturing the drink, or equal to 105,000,000 4lb. loaves.
14. 5,000 or 6,000 persons have employment found in the manufacture of the drink.*

---

* These items are derived from the following sources:—
No. 1. 17,733 drinkshops × by £750 gives £13,299,750.
,, 2. See Report of Poor Law Boards for 1869-70, page 279.
,, 3. ,, ,, ,, ,, ,, ,, 201.
,, 4. This item is assumed. See chapter on Pauperism.
,, 5. See Miscellaneous Statistics for 1869, page 140.
,, 6. See Judicial Statistics for 1869, Part I., page 39.
,, 7. ,, ,, ,, ,, ,, ,, 22.
,, 8. ,, ,, ,, ,, ,, ,, 6.
,, 9. ,, ,, ,, ,, ,, ,, 6.
,,10. ,, ,, ,, ,, ,, ,, 2.
,,11. See Parliamentary Return for April 26, 1870, No. 187.

The statistics which are here given represent only so much of the appalling evils of intemperance as come before the public eye; a great deal, however, never comes to light; and whether we take two-thirds, three-fourths, or nine-tenths of the evils as being caused by drink, we need make no abatement from the list which has been given, for the cases which are never made public will much more than make up for any allowance of this kind.

Many evils do not come to light.

From data which will be found in the chapter succeeding this, it will be seen that the indirect cost of drink, that is, what is needed to make good the losses arising from the use of intoxicating liquors, will equal or exceed the direct cost, or in other words, the money spent upon them. If this be so, then the yearly cost arising from the use of intoxicating liquors to Lancashire will be upwards of £26,000,000. I will, however, in order to come considerably within the mark, take the same at £18,000,000.

Indirect cost of intoxicating drinks to Lancashire

Having seen what are the results when the money is expended upon drink, let us notice what

No. 12. This item is based upon the assumption that there are four drunkards to each drinkshop, which I regard as under the mark.

„13. Assuming that the consumption of grain is in proportion to the intoxicating drinks used, and allowing that a bushel of grain will make 15 4lb. loaves, it gives this item.

„14. This item is assumed, as there are no returns. It does not include the sellers of liquor, but those actually employed in manufacturing it, and in manufacturing barrels, &c.

In some of these items there will probably be a difference of opinion as to the proportion attributable to drink. On this the reader must use his own judgment. My opinion is, that the evils unreported will much more than make up for any excess in the items given.

CHAP. V.

How this money should be expended.

would result if the money were appropriated in some other and better way. Let us suppose that the £18,000,000 which the drink costs Lancashire were appropriated as follows, viz: One third spent in agriculture, one third on manufactures, and the other in building houses.*

What result would accrue from this?

---

* After reading what has been adduced in reference to the value of things being only the price of the labour bestowed upon them, the reader, unless he has given the subject careful attention, may be puzzled to know why it should be that in the items of expenditure in the cases which are given, the amounts are so much greater than the sum represented in the wages. This, it will be seen, arises from the fact that the expenditure which is incurred in any manufacture, is seldom of such a kind as to embrace the whole of the labour bestowed upon the article. For instance, in the cotton trade, we start with cotton at 6d. to 9d. per lb.; these amounts represent the value of the labour expended in growing the cotton, and carrying it to this country; and then, too, there are many other things used in manufacturing, such as oil, from 4s. to 8s. per gallon, strapping at 2s. per lb., and, indeed, the whole of the machinery and material used in the mill are all articles upon which the labour has been previously expended, and which is represented in the price at which the manufacturer buys them, or in the rent he pays for them. Whilst it is true, therefore, that what we expend upon manufactured goods, or upon agricultural produce, represents labour—the labour being scattered over the entire earth may not be seen. If I resided in America, and could dig for the iron out of which to make the machinery, and could grow my own cotton, manufacture my own oil, brushes, strapping, &c., I should then employ and pay myself the whole amount of the labour expended in manufacturing the goods, it would then be seen that the price of the goods was determined by the cost of that labour. So with farming. The price at which the grain is sold (on the average) represents the labour of the farm, plus the rent, but the rent represents previous labour. The land was once waste, uncultivated land; but some one expended say £500 in improving it. This expenditure is not returned the same year, but year by year it comes back in the increased productiveness of the farm. The rent, therefore, represents this increased power of production, or, in other words, it is the return of previous labour. The same remarks apply in reference to the rents of houses and other property.

1st.—In agriculture. £6,000,000 invested in grain would purchase 17,142,852 bushels, equal to 257,142,780 4lb. loaves; it would occupy 612,600 acres of land, and would find employment for 80,000 men, at 15s. per week.

2nd. Cotton manufacturing: £6,000,000 spent upon cotton goods would purchase 6,360,000 pieces, or 468,000,000 yards of calico; which would require sixty mills, of 800 looms each, to manufacture them, and would give employment to 55,000 persons, at wages averaging for men, women, and children, 13s. 9d. per week.

Talk of bad trade! Why, at any time, if Lancashire, will only appropriate one third of its drink burden to the purchase of cotton goods, it will increase the home trade of the United Kingdom in these goods fifty per cent.

3rd.—Building houses. £6,000,000 invested in the erection of houses would build 30,996 houses, costing £150 each, and would find a year's employment for 75,000 men, at 25s. per week each. Assuming that the houses would have each a frontage of six yards, it would form a row of houses 136 miles long, or it would form two complete streets of houses stretching from Manchester to Liverpool. Here is an industial dwellings association. If all the money which intoxicating liquors cost this nation were invested in building houses, for half a dozen years, there would be a new house built for every family in the United Kingdom.

In the case of the money expended upon intoxicating drink, there is, as we have seen, at the end of the year no material return to show, but instead of this there is money wasted, food destroyed; there are drunkards, paupers, lunatics, criminals, vagrants, depredators; there are gambling-houses, brothels, houses of ill-fame, receivers of stolen goods; and following thickly in the train of these there are other evils which the pen finds it impossible to describe. As I have before stated, if the money spent upon drink (and which is virtually the price paid for these evils) were paid to get rid of them, it would be more in harmony with the dictates of reason.

In the case of the money expended upon agriculture, manufacturing, and building, there is first of all a year's employment found for 205,000 people as compared with 6,000 or 7,000 employed in the expenditure on drink. At the end of the year there is food produced equal to 257,142,780 4lb. loaves, there are 468,000,000 yards of calico manufactured, and there is a row of new houses built 136 miles long. In the case of the drink expenditure, there is the loss of £18,000,000, and no return for the same; there is also food wasted, and what is still worse, the traffic invariably leads not only to the destruction of the material wealth of the community, but also to the degradation and demoralisation of the people, We speak of production and non-production, but this trade is too ruinous to be classed under either head; it is a destroyer, and its ruinous influence blasts both the material and moral wealth of the people.

CHAP. V.
The money spent in drink would be wisely spent if paid to get rid of the evils of drinking.

The two expenditures contrasted.

It will not need more than a moment's reflection to see that in the second year of her reformed expenditure Lancashire would be much better off than in the first. She would have the £18,000,000 savings of the first year, plus the accumulated savings of the second; or, in other words, she would therefore (if her consumption had not increased) have twice as much to expend in the second year as in the first. In the third year it will be still greater, and so year by year the process goes on, and must continue to go on, for the simple reason that human labour, when properly directed, creates wealth much more rapidly than it can be consumed, if it be only applied to the rational wants of the community.

If adopted an accumulative increase of wealth would follow.

If the observations of this chapter are founded in truth, the reader will see that in a well conducted nation, such a thing as destitution or want could scarcely exist, because the labour of mankind, when rightly applied, produces so much in excess of their wants, that there must be a manifold surplus to make up for what is short during those periods of our existence when in infancy or through old age, sickness or misfortune, we are unable to produce what is needed for our maintenance and comfort. In spite, however, of these bountiful arrangements, numbers of our population are sunk in perpetual pauperism, and a large number of others are constantly on the verge thereof, whilst in many of our great towns great numbers of our skilled artizans are starving for want of

If men acted rightly, pauperism would be impossible.

employment. In a properly regulated community such a state of things could not exist, as that some of its people should be destitute of the comforts, and even of the necessaries, of life; whilst, at the same time, those whose employment consisted in providing for their wants should be pining for want of something to do. Why do these two elements so adapted to each other not meet? It can only be because so much of the material result of labour, which should reproduce itself, is destroyed, and therefore the reproductive demand is annihilated; and we have the strange spectacle of one class of the population starving for want of food and work, and another class, idling and starving for lack of the labour which should provide the food and clothing. If the reader has not already discovered the cause of this, let him read carefully the succeeding chapters.

CHAPTER VI.

ON THE MAIN CAUSE OF BAD TRADE AND NATIONAL WASTE.

A MOMENT'S reflection will make it clear to the thoughtful mind, that the reduced home demand for cotton goods, and for goods generally, must arise from one of two causes. Either we as a nation spend our money upon other things, or we have become poorer, and have not the money to spend. *Cause of reduced home demand for goods.*

We are acknowleged to be by far the richest nation in the world; and yet a great portion of our population are in rags. Why is this? Is it because they get insufficient wages that they are poor? No! for wages are relatively higher in England than almost in any country in the world; but it is because they squander their earnings improvidently upon things that are not only needless, but useless and hurtful. Let us see how far this assertion is borne out by facts. *Arises from improvidence.*

In this chapter I propose to refer to only one item in our improvident expenditure. It is an item, however, which immeasurably surpasses all the rest. I refer to the money spent upon intoxicating liquors. *Enormous expenditure upon intoxicating liquors.*

During the four years ending 1861, the expenditure upon intoxicating liquors in the United Kingdom was as follows:—

1858	£91,049,911*
1859	95,887,393
1860	86,897,683
1861	94,942,107
Total	£368,777,094
Annual Average	£92,194,273

During the four years ending 1869, the expenditure upon intoxicating drinks was as follows:†—

1866	£113,925,458‡
1867	110,122,266
1868	113,464,874
1869	112,885,603
Total	£450,398,201
Annual Average	£112,590,550

Great increase.

Being an increase in the latter period as compared with the former of £81,621,107, or £20,405,276 per annum.

* See Appendix A.

† Those readers who may have read the author's pamphlet on the "Depression in the Cotton Trade" will notice that the amount of money given above as expended upon intoxicating liquors, is considerably more than was given in the pamphlet referred to. This arises from taking an increased estimate as to the selling prices, especially in beer. See Appendixes A and D.

‡ See Appendix D.

Bad Trade and National Waste. 81

Here is an astounding fact. In four years we spent upon intoxicating drinks £450,398,201, and yet upon cotton goods during the same period we spent (reckoning 10 per cent for retailers' profits) only £51,125,842.

Expenditure on drink and cotton goods compared.

Taking the population of the United Kingdom as given in the Statistical Abstract for 1869, at 30,838,210,* it gives for each man, woman, and child in the United Kingdom for the four years £14. 12s. 1d. as spent on drink, and only £1. 13s. 1¾d. on cotton goods; or if we take the year 1869, we have £3. 13s. 2½d. on drink, and 6s. 0½d. on cotton goods; or taking a family of five persons, we have £1. 10s. 2½d. on cotton goods, and £18. 6s. 0½d. on drink.†

Average per head and per family.

Here is the secret of our bad home trade. People cannot pour their money down their throats, and put it on their backs at the same time. During the four years (ending 1869,) we swallowed 658,347,826‡ gallons more of beer, spirits, wine, &c., than we did the four years ending 1861; but during these four years (estimating five yards of calico to the lb.), we purchased 1,308,340,000 yards less of

Enormous increase in drinking.

---

* See Statistical Abstract, page 122.

† See Appendix C.

	Gallons.		Gallons.
‡ 1858	773,315,680	1866	973,649,08
1859	817,750,491	1867	921,521,567
1860	720,314,922	1868	952,904,220¾
1861	823,256,577	1869	944,853,570¾
	3,134,637,617		3,792,985,443

F

calico;* and this falling off, as we have seen, was not compensated by an equivalent increase in woollen or linen.

From the report of the Commissioners of Inland Revenue† (published in Feb., 1870), I find that the numbers of persons engaged in selling intoxicating liquors were as follows:—

Publicans	98,009
Beersellers	52,590
Total	150,599

Making a total of 150,599, being one to every 204 of the population, or about one to every 40 houses. No marvel, that with such an overwhelming amount of temptation, and with such an enormous number of people interested in pushing the sale of liquor, there should be such a large and increasing amount of drunkenness.

Unfortunately, however, the number of public-houses and beerhouses does not represent the total facilities for drunkenness. In the same report and on the same page is given a list of auxiliary sellers of intoxicating drinks, the influence of some of which is proving to be even more pernicious than public-houses or beer-shops. The following is the list‡ :—

* From a table previously given (see page 49) it will be seen that the total weight of cleaned cotton used in the home trade for the four years ending 1861 was 736,863,000 lbs.; for the four years ending 1869 it was 475,195,000 lbs.; being a falling off during the latter years of 261,668,000 lbs., and reckoning five yards to the lb. it gives 1,308,340,000 yards as stated above.

† See page 53.

DEALERS:

Spirit Dealers	5,894
Beer Dealers	5,952
Wine Dealers	3,639
Sweets — Dealers and Makers	123

RETAILERS:

Retailers of Wine (not to be consumed on the premises)	4,780
Refreshment-house keepers selling Wine	2,974
Sweets—Retailers	9,024
Packet-boat licences for sale thereon	374
Tablebeer Sellers	2,720
Retail Brewers	17
TOTAL	35,497

Making a grand total of persons engaged in selling intoxicating liquors of 186,096, or one to every thirty-three houses.

In addition to these overwhelming temptations, provision was made, by a law passed in 1862, whereby occasional licences could be taken out in order to accommodate fairs, races, shows, &c.; thus every facility has been given to spread intemperance, and every possible temptation has been placed in the way of the people, in order to lure them into habits of drunkenness.

Special licenses for fairs.

Chap. vi.
Increase in drunkenness.

No wonder, therefore, that intemperance should increase. From the Judicial Statistics for 1865* and 1869† (now lying before me), I find that the apprehensions for drunkenness for the last seven years have been as follow:

1863	94,745
1864	100,067
1865	105,310
1866	104,368
1867	100,357
1868	111,465
1869	122,310

Showing a gradual and very considerable increase in the intemperance of the country, and unmistakably proving the folly and mischief resulting from recent legislation in reference to the Wine Licence Bill, &c.

The argument good apart from Total Abstinence.

The question as to the utility of alcoholic liquors as beverages is one I will not here discuss; I believe that science and experience have both decided in favour of the total abstainer. But, apart altogether from this question, and admitting the statement as to the good of these drinks to be all that is said, there is no sane person who will plead for the spending of one hundred and ten millions a year upon them. One-fourth of this amount would be amply abundant to supply any supposed reasonable requirements; the other three-fourths represents the excess, or what results from intem-

* See page xvi.   † See page xvii.

perance, the bitter consequences of which we daily reap in the crime, pauperism, social misery, and degradation of our people.

The different ways in which the enormous expenditure upon intoxicating drinks wastes our wealth and injures our trade are too numerous fully to specify, but we will point out a few of them.

1st. Its influence on the Labour market:—

To illustrate this, I will state a fact. In the *Scotsman* newspaper for January 2nd, 1869, there is a description of the Caledonian distillery at Edinburgh.

In this distillery we learn that 40,000 gallons of spirits are manufactured weekly, or 2,000,000 per annum. At 15s. per gallon (the retail price is 20s. or more), this would be £1,500,000. The quantity of grain consumed yearly is 800,000 bushels. The number of men employed is stated to be 150.

Now, if the £1,500,000 were spent upon manufactured goods, or in building houses, or in draining waste land, it would give employment to from 12,000 to 15,000 persons, or more; and if the whole amount which is wasted upon drink by us as a nation, were thus spent, it would find employment for at least 1,500,000 more persons than are at present engaged. Here then is an answer to the question—What shall be done with our surplus population? Not send them as emigrants to other countries, but by spending our money judiciously we should find them abundant work at home; we should have work for all, and to spare.

Strange! marvellously strange! that men of intelligence cannot see this. They go on forming emigration societies, sending our best workmen—who above all others should stay at home—out of the country; and housing in workhouses and goals, a whole host of paupers and criminals, made so by drink. If three-fourths of the money spent on intoxicating liquors were spent upon clothing, furniture, or in the erection of houses, &c., it would give full employment for all our idlers; and, besides this, pauperism itself, as well as crime, with all their attendant evils, would rapidly diminish, or altogether disappear; and those perplexing problems of our legislation, which are a disgrace to our Christianity and our civilization, would be solved; and most of the social evils we have so bitterly to mourn would be eradicated.

2nd. Another way in which the expenditure upon intoxicating liquors wastes the national wealth and injures our trade, is by degrading our population to paupers and criminals, for it will be readily seen that by so doing it not only increases our taxation, but also by throwing such large numbers of our population out of employment, also greatly diminishes the productive power of our industries.

The amount paid for Poor and Police Rates during the ten years ending 1869 has been as follows:—*

---

* See Statistical Abstract, page 128.

Bad Trade and National Waste.

Tabular View of the Amount of Poor and Police Rates paid during each Year from 1860 to 1869 inclusive.

	England and Wales.	Scotland.	Ireland.	Total.
	£	£	£	£
1860	8,075,904	663,277	530,626	9,269,807
1861	8,395,212	683,902	595,192	9,674,306
1862	8,806,074	719,317	652,245	10,177,636
1863	9,325,071	736,028	701,031	10,762,130
1864	9,680,180	770,030	732,968	11,183,478
1865	9,792,193	778,274	736,629	11,307,096
1866	9,989,121	783,127	726,340	11,498,588
1867	10,905,173	807,631	797,134	12,509,938
1868	11,380,593	863,202	841,512	13,085,307
1869	11,773,999	931,275	836,553	13,541,827

Poor and Police rates from 1860 to 1869.

From these tables it will be seen, that the number of paupers and the consequent expense have been gradually increasing, year by year, until on the first of January, 1870 .(estimating Scotland as in 1869), our paupers numbered 1,281,651, and the poor and police rates reached the frightful sum of £13,541,827. Or if we take another view, whilst in 1869 we only paid £8,501,737 for cotton goods, we paid for poor and police rates, £13,541,827, being £5,040,090 more for poor rates, &c., than the entire total of our home consumption of cotton goods.

Expenditure on cotton goods and Poor rates.

If it were not for the liquor traffic, our rates need not, at the outside, be more than a fourth of what they now are, and thus a sum of about ten millions yearly might be available for our trade. If during the last few years this amount had been

Taxation injures trade.

appropriated to the purchase of cotton goods, our home consumption would have been nearly doubled and the cotton trade would not have been in such a deplorable condition as it has been. The question of intemperance becomes therefore vastly important, not only as a matter of direct expenditure, but also as one of local and national taxation.

I have often heard it stated, and there is considerable truth in the statement, that, owing to the heavy local taxation in Manchester, and other large towns, spinners and manufacturers find it impossible to compete with country mills, where the taxation is lighter; and hence it is observed that, whilst no new mills are being built in Manchester, old ones are being stopped, and the trade is gradually shifting to more lightly taxed regions.

What is true of different districts in the same country, is equally true of different countries; the rates which a manufacturer has to pay must come out of trade profits, which makes the production of goods more expensive; and, consequently, other things being equal, if a large mill is taxed at the rate of £500 per annum in this country, but only £100 on the Continent, the Continental manufacturer has the advantage of £400 per annum over his English competitor.

The argument which is applicable to taxation is equally applicable to wasteful expenditure, which is nothing but self-imposed taxation. A mill employing 500 workpeople would represent a population of 800 persons. As has been shown, we tax ourselves annually in our expenditure upon drink to the amount of £3. 13s. 2½d. per head, which, in a mill employing 500 workpeople, and representing a population of 800 people, amounts to a tax of over £2,900 per annum.

Indeed, if the money were paid as a direct tax, the consequences would be far less pernicious, because, in this case, the payment of the tax would be the sum total of the evil; but when the money is spent on drink, additional and most deplorable evils follow; evils that bring in their train vice, wretchedness, and social demoralization, that are truly appalling. *Compulsory taxation least hurtful.*

But losing sight altogether of these attendant social evils, the argument used in reference to the self-imposed taxation is equally pertinent in its application to trade as in the case of the compulsory tax; and if a compulsory tax of £500 per annum places a mill at so much disadvantage, what must be the influence of a self-imposed tax of over £2,900 per annum? In both cases the tax must be paid out of the profits of trade, and hence it acts as a perpetual drawback upon us, crippling our resources, and placing us at so much of a disadvantage compared with other nations, which have not the same wasteful expenditure. *All taxes come out of trade profits.*

3rd. The loss to the nation which results from the pauperism and crime of the country, unfortunately, however, is not confined merely to the sum necessary to maintain paupers and punish criminals. If these people were industriously *Wealth lost through enforced idleness.*

employed, their industry would add to the riches of the community; instead, however, of reaping the benefits of such industry, society has to support them in idleness, and has also to make good the mischief arising from their criminal acts.

How capital is abstracted. 4th. The expenditure on drink injures our trade also, by abstracting capital from the country. Were it not for the grain destroyed in brewing and distillation, we should need little or none of the grain that has to be imported. The money paid to foreign countries would, therefore, be available for home use. Besides this, there is the money paid to other countries for wines, spirits, sugar used in brewing, distillation, &c., all of which, if not thus foolishly spent, might be laid out upon our own home trade, thus accumulating our riches, stimulating our manufactures, and finding employment for our artizans.

5th. Another way in which the liquor traffic injures trade and commerce is by involving the destruction of a large amount of grain, thereby causing food to be dear, and as the use of food is a matter of necessity the purchase of manufactured goods becomes of secondary importance; any increase, therefore, in the price of food, diminishes proportionably the sum available for the purchase of clothing, &c.

The amount of grain destroyed in the manufacture of intoxicating drinks in the year 1869 was as follows:—

Bad Trade and National Waste.

	BUSHELS.
Malt used in brewing*	47,704,819
Sugar used in brewing 342,678 cwts., equal to†	1,462,092
Corn used in making 21,941,779 gallons of spirits,‡ reckoning 18 gallons to 8 bushels	9,751,901
61,792§ acres of the best land used for growing hops for brewing purposes, at 30 bushels per acre, would give	1,853,760
Produce destroyed in making cider, perry, British wines, &c., say‖	2,000,000
	62,772,572

This statement does not include the destruction of grain and vegetable produce involved in the manufacture of 8,172,845¶ gallons of foreign spirits, and of 14,734,534 gallons of wine. If the grain thus destroyed, or its equivalent in produce be calculated in grain, and added to the above, it will give at least a total of 70,000,000 bushels of grain or produce destroyed in manufacturing the intoxicating liquors consumed in one year in this country. A bushel of malt is equivalent to a bushel of barley,

No. of loaves the grain would make.

---

* See Trade and Navigation Returns for year ending Dec. 31, 1869, page 51.

† See Trade and Navigation Returns for year ending Dec. 31, 1869, page 51.

‡ See Trade and Navigation Returns for year ending Dec. 31, 1869, page 51.

§ See Statistical Abstract, page 111.

‖ This amount is assumed, as there are no published statistics.

¶ See Statistical Abstract for 1870, page 49.

which weighs 53lb., and will give at least 40lb. of flour, which will make 60lb.* of bread, or 15 4lb. loaves per bushel, making a grand total of grain or produce destroyed equal to 1,050,000,000 four-pound loaves, or about 170 loaves yearly for every family of five persons throughout the United Kingdom.

Length of road these loaves would pave

No. of carts it would take to cart them away.

If these loaves were used as paving stones, they would pave a road 10 yards wide more than 1,800 miles long, or above nine times the distance from London to Manchester. If the loaves had to be carted away from some baker's shop in London, and tumbled into the Thames, and one horse and cart were engaged to do it, taking 550 loaves every half hour for ten hours each day, it would take more than 330 years to cart them all away, or it would take 330 carts one year to do it.

It would be a less evil if the bread were thrown into the Thames.

What a sensation of horror it would produce, if some fine morning 330 carts, each laden with 500 loaves of bread, were to draw up to London Bridge, and the various drivers began to prepare to shunt their contents into the river. If such a thing were attempted, those who ventured upon the experiment would be quickly tumbled in after the loaves; and yet, if this were done every day during the year, and the grain were thus destroyed, instead of being destroyed by being converted into intoxicating liquors, it would be a most unspeakable blessing to the community; for, if thrown into the river, the bread would be lost,

---

* See Johnston's Chemistry of Common Life, page 98.

but that would be the end of it; as it is, it is not only lost, but converted into a maddening liquor, which ruins and destroys the people, not only as to their substance but their virtue also, and fills the land with mourning, lamentation, and woe. Better would it be to destroy only the grain than both the grain and the people.

Writers on political economy argue (and rightly) that a bad harvest causes dear food, and leads to bad trade; because people, having more to pay for food, cannot afford clothing and other comforts; but, so far as the result goes, there is no difference in the long run between 70,000,000 bushels of grain destroyed by bad weather, and 70,000,000 destroyed in the manufacture of liquor. In both cases the food is abstracted from the market, which causes prices to rise; and in the latter case, in addition to the destruction of the grain, there is the destruction of the people's morality, and burdens and evils entailed that are immeasurable.

It is clear, therefore, that if the grain used in brewing and distillation were used in baking, we should have a far more plentiful supply, bread would, therefore, be cheaper, and, as a consequence, people needing to pay less for food would have more for clothing; our trade would therefore be augmented. Thus in a multitude of ways, it is clear that our bad trade has arisen, not from a bad foreign demand, but from a deficient home trade, arising entirely from our squandering our money upon things not only useless, but things

CHAP. VI.

How our workmen are deteriorated.

which are pernicious, and which in all their subsequent relations and results, continue to injure our trade and commerce, and also to demoralize our population.

6th. The liquor traffic injures trade and decreases our national wealth also, by unsettling our industrial relations, and deteriorating the character of our workmen. People who are wishful to invest money, especially in business which necessitates the employment of a number of workmen, are often deterred from doing so by the fear of the trouble which they are likely to have, owing to the intemperate and unsteady character of the workmen. In this way industry is often checked, and the extension of trade prevented.

But it is not only by checking the development of trade that the evil of intemperance operates, but it operates, too, most perniciously in the carrying on of each trade. Let a man have a mill or a workshop of any kind fitted up with machinery, one part dependent upon another, and all dependent very greatly upon the skill and steadiness of the workmen, the acceptance of orders, too, being dependent upon their prompt and skilful execution—if such a man often finds eight or ten out of every hundred workmen away drinking, the machinery standing idle whilst he is keeping the engine going to turn it, he will be a great loser; the work will neither be done in quality nor quantity as it ought to be, and therefore the intemperate habits of the workman are a great loss and drawback to him. If there is any danger at all to British industry and commerce, it arises from the superior intelligence and sobriety of the continental workman as compared with our own. If the British workman be at all inferior in these respects, it entirely arises from the habits of intemperance to which he is addicted.

Intemperance the great source of danger.

7th. The liquor traffic injures trade and wastes the national wealth, also, by the loss of life and property which it occasions.

The goods manager of one of the railways running into Manchester told the writer, that the line of which he was manager paid no less a sum than £5,000 annually in consequence of accidents and damages, which could clearly be traced to drunkenness. How many other accidents occurred which could not be so traced, he observed that he could not tell. The case of this line is but a sample of what is occurring over the entire country—everywhere, railway collisions, colliery accidents, boiler explosions, and numerous other accidents, upon a lesser scale, are constantly occurring; whilst cases of personal violence, or murder, or premature death, especially of children, who perish through the neglect of their parents, or, as is often the case, are overlain and suffocated by them whilst in a state of drunkenness, are so common, as almost to pass unnoticed; indeed the mischief and peril resulting to life and property through intemperance are incalculable, rendering life and property insecure, and enormously increasing all manner of risks, and not only destroying existing wealth, but paralyzing the sinews of industry so as to retard its development in the future.

In the estimates I have given as to the cost of intoxicating liquors, I have taken into account only the money directly spent in their purchase: unfortunately, this only partially represents the cost to the nation. In their train follow unparalleled losses and evils which fall upon society; and therefore in taking a proper estimate of this total loss, it is necessary not only that the direct but also the indirect cost be included.

The Rev. D. Burns, M.A., on the indirect loss of wealth through intoxicating liquors.

The Rev. Dawson Burns, M.A., of London, than whom there is no better authority upon a question of this nature, estimates this indirect loss as follows :—

First.—Loss of wealth annually incurred in the production and retailing of intoxicating liquors :—

1. The land now devoted to the growth of barley and hops, used in making intoxicating liquors, would produce food of the value of not less than . £13,000,000
2. In the manufacture of strong drink there is a loss of capital and labour worth at least . . 15,000,000
3. The labour of the retailer of intoxicating drinks and of their servants, numbering 500,000 or upwards, would be worth, at the low estimate of £50 each per annum 25,000,000

Total £53,000,000

Second.—Expenses and burdens annually arising from the use of intoxicating liquors:—

1. Loss of labour and time to employers and workmen by drinking,—estimated by the Parliamentary Committee of 1834 at £50,000,000
2. Destruction of property by sea and land, and loss of property by theft and otherwise, the result of drinking habits, say . 10,000,000
3. Public and private charges by pauperism, destitution, sickness, insanity, and premature deaths, traceable to the use of strong drinks, at least . . . 10,000,000
4. Cost of police, prosecutions, courts of justice, support of criminals, losses by jurors and witnesses,—taking the proportion of cases due to drinking, at least 3,000,000

£73,000,000

Third.—Add amount of money directly spent on intoxicating liquors in 1869 112,885,603

Grand total of the yearly loss of wealth to the British Nation through intoxicating drinks £238,885,603

This calculation, of course, is only an estimate, and the intelligent reader will enlarge or curtail it as in his judgment appears requisite. My own opinion is that the two last items might without any exaggeration be made 10,000,000 more, and that if a proper allowance were made for the lost labour of our paupers, criminals, vagrants, thieves, lunatics, &c., it would amount to at least £20,000,000 more, which would make a total of £268,885,603. Under any circumstances, however, we shall be considerably within the mark in assuming, that the direct and indirect cost to the nation, arising from the use of intoxicating liquors, cannot be less than £200,000,000 yearly—a sum equal to nearly one-fourth of the income of the entire nation!

What a deplorable fact it is to contemplate, that an enlightened and professedly Christian nation, should spend £200,000,000 per annum in bringing upon itself misery, impoverishment, degradation, and demoralisation. If the money were paid to remove these evils, it would be a rational expenditure, but when the evils are bought, and at such an enormous cost, reason and common sense—not to mention religion—stand aghast in mute astonishment, totally unable to realise the possibility of such insane folly.

At the Annual Meeting of the Manchester Chamber of Commerce, held in the autumn of 1869, Sir Thomas Bazley, addressing the Chamber, said:—"When he looked at the deprivations which the labouring classes had sustained, the diminution of the capital of the employing classes, the devastations in the money market produced by limited liability and undue speculations, and added to those disasters the dearness of food which prevailed for two years after the termination of the American war, he came to the conclusion that the vast sum of 250 millions sterling had been abstracted from the resources of the country; and he was only surprised that the financial and commercial systems of the country had sustained the great and pressing weight that had encumbered them. He did not wonder at the complaint that trade was embarrassed and unprofitable, nor at the complaint that orders for manufactures of every kind were difficult to obtain; for it was clear that if, during seven years, the sum of 250 millions sterling had been taken from the ordinary expenditure of the country, not only the cotton trade, but also every other trade, must have been deprived of the means of purchasing an immense amount of the manufactures that were produced by the various industries of the country."

Losses through seven years of dear food, &c.

Now, if the loss of £250,000,000 through dear food, &c., during seven years, tends so much to embarrass and render trade unprofitable, what influence must the loss of £1,400,000,000, through intemperance, have upon it? Is there something peculiar and exceptional in the money that is lost through drink that prevents it from damaging trade? Has it not the same effect that other losses have? Yes, and worse; for there is not only a money loss, but there is also the deterioration and demoralisation of the workman, which is the greatest loss of all. Why, then, do not our

Losses through seven years of intemperance.

statesmen, our political economists, and our commercial magnates draw attention to this as well as other causes of bad trade? They must see these things, unless they shut their eyes and will not see. If so, they stand convicted of withholding the truth out of deference to the depraved habits of the community. With such men at the helm, the national ship stands in great danger of being wrecked.

It is not unfrequently objected, and the objection sometimes comes from men of intelligence and men conversant with trade, that inasmuch as, notwithstanding the large expenditure arising from drink, trade has often been good in the past, and doubtless ere long may again be good in the future, the argument, therefore, that this expenditure leads to bad trade falls to the ground.

There has never, however, been a period when the expenditure upon intoxicating drinks has been so large as during the four years ending 1869. During those four years (as we have seen) it was twenty millions per annum more than during the four years ending 1861, and therefore the experiences of former years does not apply to the present. If, however, it did, and the premises were admitted, the conclusion by no means follows.

If a man possesses an income of £500 per annum he may squander £450 of it, and not suffer from it: if however his income be reduced to £400, and his expenditure increased to £500, he will soon find himself in difficulties. When such an one gets into difficulties, it is absurd for him to plead the

Individuals or Nations, with large incomes may be extravagant.

reduction of his income as an excuse for his troubles, the cause lies in his extravagance. So it is with nations.

CHAP. VI.

When a nation, by its inventive genius, by its skill and industry, by its unrivalled machinery, its unbounded mineral wealth, its humid climate, and its happy situation, has been raised to such a position as to have become to a great extent the workshop of the world, it thereby for the time being enjoys a monopoly, and secures to itself such an income as enables it to act very lavishly in regard to its expenditure.

Our exceptional opportunities for getting wealth.

No nation, however, can long expect to enjoy a monopoly of such advantages; and if it fosters habits of intemperance, it must, when circumstances become less propitious, be involved in difficulties. Under such circumstances there will be only one of two courses open, either to give up its indulgences, or reduce its trade.

This cannot always last.

Such has been our position during the last few years. Owing to the high price of much of our raw material for manufactures, dear food, the failure of joint stock associations, &c., the profits of trade latterly have been very greatly reduced, and we have for a time been deprived of those special facilities for money making, which for a long period we have so pre-eminently enjoyed. This, however, has not led to a reduction in our expenditure upon indulgences. Our expenditure upon intoxicating drinks instead of diminishing has increased, and therefore, as an inevitable

These facilities have latterly been reduced.

But drinking has increased.

consequence, the expenditure upon other things must be diminished. The experience of the last few years testifies that such has been the case. The only way, therefore, to improve trade, so far as the home department is concerned, is to transfer the expenditure now appropriated to drink to useful articles of manufacture.

Evils of scarcity of the raw material for manufacturing.

It is doubtless true, that when there is a scarcity in the raw material in any manufacture, that kind of manufacture can never be so healthy as it otherwise would be, but, it is clear, that if the enormous amount expended upon drink were saved, whenever such scarcity did arise we should be in a far better position to cope with it than we now are—for, 1st, we should be very much richer, and therefore more able to bid for the raw material in the markets of the world—more of it would consequently come to this country, and our mills would be better employed; and, 2nd, our workpeople, were they sober, would rapidly save money, and they would be able to put up with short time without inconvenience. We might then, with comfort to all, regulate the consumption to the supply, and secure a far steadier, and more profitable trade than we could otherwise enjoy.

How temperance would ameliorate these evils.

During the American war people were afraid to grow cotton, for fear the war should suddenly collapse, and the three or four million bales which were thought to be locked up in the Southern States, should be let loose, and swamp the market. For three or four years after the termination of the war, the fearful stagnation which prevailed in the Manchester market drove all heart out of capitalists. Cotton, it was said, must come down, for people will not pay the prices for cloth; hence, in the autumn of 1867, middling Orleans cotton fell to 7d. per lb. The consequence was that the growth of the staple was checked, and the period of cotton scarcity has been prolonged one or two years further than it otherwise would have been.

The influence of low prices on the growth of cotton.

How was it likely prices could be maintained, when our own home trade had fallen off thirty-five per cent? and how was it likely that merchants would push the growth of an article for which there was so little demand?

Cause of the depression in the price of cotton.

Had the twenty millions spent upon drink during the four years ending 1869, in excess of that spent in the four years ending 1861, or had even one-half of it been spent upon cotton goods, it would have more than doubled our home trade, and thus have kept up a healthy demand for goods; as a consequence, cotton would have maintained its value, the world would have been encouraged to push on its growth, and very much earlier than has been the case, we should have had a full supply.

These evils would be mitigated by temperance.

Mr. R. Dudley Baxter, in his work on "The Taxation of the United Kingdom," remarks, "A commercial people, who depend for their market upon the cheapness of their production, can afford no waste."

This, in the long run, is sure to prove true, for whatever unnecessary waste there may be, operates as so much of a bonus to competitors, and ultimately, if continued, enables them to supplant us in the world's market, provided they do not imitate our folly.

Results which follow from careful industry.

The invention of the steam engine, the spinning jenny, the loom, and other valuable machines, has for a long time placed in our hands a monopoly of wealth; our coal fields, iron mines, &c., have supplemented these; and had we been wise, and during the last fifty years properly husbanded and used the wealth thus placed within our reach, our people to-day would universally have been in easy circumstances, and we should have been far from the fearful pauperism that marks us as a disgrace among the nations of the earth.

As I have previously intimated, there has never been a nation in the world's history, whose opportunities for acquiring wealth have been equal to those possessed by ourselves. Enjoying, as we do, a vast commerce with every region of the globe, and possessing manufacturing advantages and facilities far surpassing those of any other nation, this country has, to a great extent, become the workshop of the world. When a nation possesses no resources but such as are within itself, it may, even then, if it uses those resources aright, rapidly accumulate wealth; but when, in addition to its own resources, it enjoys the advantage of being enriched by the trade of every country in the world, its progress ought to be such as to lift it far above the regions of want; and such would be ours, if it were not for the fearful drawbacks and waste of intemperance.

The burden of taxation, crime, pauperism, and demoralisation that results from the liquor traffic every day becomes more and more oppressive; and the time is fast hastening when, if we do not grapple with the evil, we shall sink beneath its weight, and take our place in the second or third rank among the nations of the earth. Persia, Babylon, Carthage, Greece, Rome, Spain, and other kingdoms which once were in the front rank, have played their part, and now are scarcely known except in history. It was their profligacy, extravagance, and debauchery which sank them, and ours will sink us, not only commercially, but morally and religiously, unless we adopt means to prevent them.

What results from profligacy.

The remedy for our bad trade, then, lies entirely with ourselves. If we think we can continue to squander one hundred millions yearly on drink, increasing thereby very materially our local taxation and sapping the foundations of industry, virtue, and morality, we shall be greatly mistaken.

We may have an abundant and prosperous trade, we may ensure to our artisans, and our industrial population, continued, and profitable employment, we may free our country from the fearful stains of pauperism and crime which so disfigure it; we may have a wealthy, contented, virtuous, and happy people, but if we are ever to secure these

The remedy lies in removing the causes of intemperance.

CHAP. VI.

inestimable blessings we must remove the temptations to intemperance which are planted broadcast over the land; and our legislature must enact such laws as "will make it easy to do right, and difficult to do wrong."*

* "The disposition to be provident, I need not tell you, cannot be supplied by Parliament. It may be the duty of the legislature to prohibit certain things—and so it is—which are of the nature of social abuses; but, with regard to the general government of man, it has pleased God to make him a free agent, and those by whom he is ruled in this world ought to respect the freedom—ought to make it easy for him to do what is right, and difficult for him to do wrong."—*Speech of the Right Hon. W. E. Gladstone, at Buckley, Jan. 4th*, 1864.

CHAPTER VII.

ON THE RIGHT EXPENDITURE OF MONEY.

IF the reader has carefully perused Chapter V. he will see the truth of the following positions;—

I. When labour is directed to productive and useful objects, and these objects are rightly used, there will necessarily be a rapid accumulation in the products of industry.

II. That inasmuch as the value of things (commercially) is in proportion to the amount of the labour expended upon them, it follows that to purchase any object is simply to pay for the labour expended thereon, and therefore the income of one week, if properly expended, will create a demand for the labour of the succeeding one.

III. That in proportion to the accumulation of the products of industry, or in other words, of wealth, so also will be the power to employ labour; hence, in proportion as a nation increases in wealth, and uses that wealth rightly, pauperism, vagrancy, and all other evils of a kindred class must disappear.

The question as to the influence which a proper or improper expenditure of money exercises upon the demand for labour, and also upon the waste of our national resources, is one of the greatest importance; but it is one which is very imperfectly comprehended. I therefore ask the reader's careful attention whilst I dwell upon the subject, in order to elucidate what is of such pre-eminent importance.

I will revert to the illustration made use of in a previous chapter, in reference to the digging of the hole and filling it up again.

Illustration from the case of digging the hole.

Suppose the case of a man thus employed. He is engaged during the week in digging a hole, and then at the week's end he fills it up again, for doing which he is paid fifteen shillings as wages. Some one may perhaps say, the man who has got his fifteen shillings, by re-spending it, can find some one else a week's work on the same terms as he himself has been employed. But then, in considering this question, it must be borne in mind that there are two persons concerned in the business of the hole digging,—there is the employer, as well as the employed,—there is the man who paid the fifteen shillings, as well as the man who received it. The employer gave his money and the workman gave his labour. The workman, in return for his labour, gets fifteen shillings; but what does the employer get in return for his money? He gets nothing. If the fifteen shillings were all he possessed, then the transaction reduces him to poverty, for he paid all that he had, and it produced him nothing in return.

Now, suppose that instead of spending his time in digging this hole, the man had been employed in manufacturing cloth, or in making shoes, or in cultivating land, or in any other kind of productive labour; what then would have been the result? He would have produced probably 200 or 300 yards of cloth, or two or three pairs of shoes, or perhaps twenty shillings' worth of grain: for a week's productive labour by the man would not only have reproduced the fifteen shillings, but it would have reproduced it with a profit.* The employer would have parted with his fifteen shillings, but in return for it would probably have received twenty shillings' worth of produce.

Illustration from the manufacture of shoes, &c.

Let us stop to compare the result in each case. In one case there is fifteen shillings expended, but nothing produced,—the workman gets his wages, but the employer loses his fifteen shillings; and, as I have remarked, if he is only worth fifteen shillings, he is reduced to poverty. In the second case, the workman gets his wages, and the employer gets probably twenty shillings' worth of produce, for productive expenditure and labour (which are really synonymous) reproduce themselves with a profit. In the former case there is only the fifteen shillings received by the workman; in the latter case there is the fifteen shillings which the workman gets, plus the twenty shillings which

The two results compared.

---

* In many of the calculations and arguments made use of in this treatise, the profit arising from invested wealth is not taken into account. This profit is a variable quantity, and has been omitted in order that the reasoning might not become too complicated. If it had been taken into account, the reader will see that it would have made the writer's argument all the stronger.

the employer receives, and in addition to the week's labour which the fifteen shillings earned by the workman would purchase. The employer's twenty shillings would also enable him to find some other individual 1¼ week's labour. In one case, therefore, there would be one day's labour found; and, in the other case, there would be 2¼ day's labour ensured. Whether, therefore, the expenditure be measured by the wealth it produces, or by the amount of labour it will employ, the reader will see the vast importance of its being properly directed so as to be productive.

It is no uncommon thing for people—even working men—to spend their five, ten, fifteen, or twenty shillings, in one week, in intoxicating liquors. With such men, any advance in wages is simply providing them greater facility for their own degradation. Let it be supposed that the two men we have just referred to, are of this stamp, and that instead of investing the fifteen shillings in hole-digging, they had spent it in beer or spirits, and that the man, instead of being employed at the hole, had been employed in manufacturing the same. In this case, what would be the result? Let us apply this reasoning not to a supposed case, but to one which unfortunately is of every day occurrence. I refer to the purchase of intoxicating drinks.

In manufacturing intoxicating drinks the first thing that the man has to do, is, to get some of the best grain he can, whether it be for brewing or distillation.* To make fifteen shillings' worth of beer, he would have to use as much grain as would make six 4lb. loaves. The time he would be employed in manufacturing the beer would not be a couple of hours—I will assume it however to be a quarter of a day—this, at fifteen shillings per week, would give the workman 7½d. as wages. How then stands the matter? At the beginning of the week the men had fifteen shillings in cash, which they expended in beer. To make this beer, three shillings' worth of grain has to be used (reckoning grain only at six shillings per bushel), and there is a quarter of a day's employment found, for which 7½d. goes into the pocket of the workman as wages. They are therefore richer by the 7½d., but they are poorer (so far as the result of this transaction is concerned) by the fifteen shillings spent on the beer, plus the three shillings' worth of grain destroyed in its manufacture. If such extravagant conduct as this was not atoned for by the industry and providence of others, what would such men

margin notes: What results from fifteen shillings spent in beer. — The provident have to atone for the prodigal.

* The following quantities have been found to afford a good product of whiskey in a well-conducted Scotch distillery:—

252	bushels of malt,	at	40lbs.	per bushel.
948	,,	barley,	53¾lbs.	,,
150	,,	oats,	47¼lbs.	,,
150	,,	rye,	53¾lbs.	,,
1500				

From each bushel of the above mixed meal 2¼ gallons of proof whiskey may be obtained, or 18¾ gallons per quarter. A few distillers are skilful enough to extract 20 gallons per quarter from such a mixture.—*English Encyclopædia.* Article—Distillery.

have to do? How could they get a second week's job? They have only 7½d. wherewith to provide for it. This illustration will show that the reason why so many of our population are out of employment, and cannot get it, is owing to the unproductive and wasteful manner in which money is expended upon intoxicating liquors.

The point now under discussion is one of the most vital importance. I will therefore, in order to exhibit more fully its influence upon society generally, take an illustration upon a more extended scale.

Illustration drawn from the Poor Law Union of Bury.

I will take, as my first illustration, the Poor-Law Union of Bury, in which I reside. The population of the Union in 1861 was 101,132. Out of this number, there will be about 50,000 persons who are engaged in labour of some kind or other. I will assume that this labour is properly directed so as to be all productive, and that their average earnings amount to 14s. each per week, or a total for the entire population (allowing two weeks for holidays) of £1,750,000 per annum. The rest of the population—consisting of mothers, young children, aged and infirm people—are unable to work, and have, therefore, to be maintained by the labour of the 50,000 workers.

The value of goods is the labour expended upon them.

As I have before shown, if the raw material for manufacture were all found within the area of the Bury district, then the value of the manufactures when sold would represent simply the value of the labour expended upon them—or, in other words, the wages paid to the workpeople. In most districts, however, this is only the case to a very limited extent, the material generally coming from other districts, and the price paid for it representing the labour which has been spent upon it in those districts. In these cases, therefore, the value of the article when sold will represent the price paid for the material imported, plus the labour expended upon it in the district where its manufacture is completed. Thus, in the Bury district, if £1,750,000 be the wages paid, it will probably represent articles which, when sold, will fetch say, £3,500,000. Of this £3,500,000, one-half is paid for the material of manufacture when it comes to Bury, and the other represents the wages paid upon it in Bury. These two items added together, therefore, will constitute its selling price.

This, the reader will see, is exactly the same in principle as in the case where the manufacture is begun and completed within the district.

In order, however, that the illustration may not be encumbered by any foreign considerations, I will suppose that Bury is so situated as to possess a sufficient area to grow its own produce; also, that it possesses within itself all the raw material for its manufactures. In such a case, what wealth it possesses will clearly depend upon the industry of its 50,000 workers.

A case supposed.

If the labours of these 50,000 people are properly apportioned and directed so as to be productive, there would be, say, about 10,000 engaged in

How labour should be divided.

providing food, 20,000 in providing clothing and other manufactures, and 20,000 would be employed in building houses, making furniture, &c. Under these three heads might be comprised, all classes of productive labour and expenditure, so that for every pound expended there would be its equivalent returned in value to the purchaser, and for every day's labour its equivalent in wealth.

I will suppose that on the 1st of January, 1870, the population referred to had, either in money or produce, a year's income in hand, upon which they are to subsist during 1870, whilst they make provision for 1871.

The reader will bear in mind that in this argument, I have assumed that the district has all its resources entirely within itself, and that those resources are productively employed. In such a region wealth must rapidly accumulate; everybody who wishes to work must be fully employed; whilst pauperism and destitution can have no existence. Unfortunately, such a state of things does not exist. We must, therefore, consider things as they are, and note what are the main hindrances to the consummation so devoutly to be wished.

No. of public-houses and beerhouses in the Bury Union.

In the Bury Union* there are 205 public-houses, and 295 beershops, or a total of 500 places where intoxicating liquors are sold, in addition to a num-

* The population in the Bury Poor-Law Union is about three times as great as in the Borough—it includes a number of the out-lying townships.

ber of grocers who, since 1860, have begun to sell wines and spirits. It has been shown that the average expenditure for each of these houses throughout the United Kingdom is upwards of £750 per annum. Assuming that Bury does its share of this expenditure, it will give a total of £375,000* as spent upon intoxicating liquors in one year, or upwards of a fifth of its total income. What are the results which follow from this expenditure?

It has been previously shown that in the manufacture of intoxicating liquors very little labour is required; that between the duty paid to Government, the price paid for the grain destroyed, and the enormous profits derived by the brewers and publicans, there is very little left for wages to the working man. The manufacture of £375,000 worth of intoxicating liquors would not at the outside employ more than from 200 to 250 people; and if to these be added the 500 publicans, and say as many servants, it would give 1,000 persons more, who, though not engaged in the manufacture, yet are maintained by the money spent. This would be a total of 1,250 persons, (a very outside estimate) who derive a living from the £375,000 expended upon drink.

Small amount of labour needed in the manufacture of drink.

---

* It may perhaps be objected that this amount is excessive. All I have to say in reply is, I give the figures as I find them. It is certainly startling, and especially when it is borne in mind that it only represents the direct expenditure. If the indirect could be added, the amount, large as it is, would have to be about doubled.—See previous Chapter, also Appendix B.

Chap. VII.

Loss of labour in Bury through drink.

Now, if £1,750,000 will give employment to 50,000, it follows that, if properly expended, £375,000 would find employment and subsistence for 10,714 persons, or 9,464 more than when spent on drink; so that by spending so much of the money on drink there are, out of the 50,000 workers, 9,464 who are thrown out of employment, and have to be supported by the labour of the other 40,536 workers.

Loss of grain.

But the spending of £375,000 upon intoxicating drinks involves also the destruction of at least 250,000 bushels of grain, which, if converted into bread, would make above three and a half million 4lb. loaves, and would provide sustenance during the whole year for at least one fourth of the population in the union. If the liquor could be manufactured out of some material that could be had for nothing, and which, by expending labour upon it, could be converted into intoxicating liquor, so that the price of the liquor represented the price of the labour, then, so far as the labour question went, it would be on a par with the case of digging the hole and filling it up again; it would simply be the loss of the labour. But, unfortunately, the labour of the drink manufacture is much worse than this: it is not only unproductive, but destructive, for an amount of food which would sustain one fourth of the population, is wasted, in order to manufacture a pernicious liquor.

When we compare the results which accrue to the community from the two methods of expenditure, we find that when the £1,750,000 is expended without any of it going for the purchase of intoxicating liquors, 50,000 persons derive productive employment; but when the 500 public-houses and beer shops are established, and £375,000 of the money goes in drink, then, only 40,536 persons are employed, and out of these 1,250 are not only unproductively, but destructively employed; or to put the thing in another light, when the money is expended without the drink, there are 50,000 individuals who are productively employed, but when £375,000 of it is expended in drink, there are only 39,286 employed productively, whilst 1,250 are employed in destroying what the 39,286 create; for, as we have seen, each year they destroy grain that would provide bread equivalent to three and a half million 4lb. loaves, whilst a fifth of the people are thrown out of employment, and have to be provided for by the industry of the others. Here is the explanation for the fearful amount of pauperism, vagrancy, and destitution which exists. Spend the money properly, and, with our present industry, confirmed pauperism would be an impossibility.

It has been correctly remarked by Professor Fawcett* that, "Although no wealth whatever can be produced without labour, yet there is much labour which does not contribute to the creation of wealth." Professor Fawcett might have gone further than this; he might have added—there is much labour which contributes to the destruction of wealth.

* Manual of Political Economy. page 13.

CHAP. VII.
A comparison to illustrate mis-spent money.

If a man could be so foolish as to pull his house down in order to erect a pig-stye upon its site, then the price of the pig-stye, if it is to represent its cost, must include, not only the value of the labour expended in erecting the stye, but also, the value of the labour expended in erecting the house pulled down to make room for the stye, and also the cost of pulling it down. At least, therefore, nineteen-twentieths of the cost of the stye, is what is paid to atone for this destructive labour.

Cost value and utility value illustrated.

In the above case nineteen-twentieths of the cost of the pig-stye, would be the price paid to make up for the destruction of the house. The utility value is merely the cost of erecting the stye; but the value of cost, or labour, is the price paid for building up, and also pulling down the house, plus the cost of building the stye. The money it takes to erect the house, pull it down, and erect the stye, indicates the cost value, and in all cases, in proportion as the cost value exceeds the utility value, by so much does the world become impoverished, because labour is expended that does not return a corresponding value of use.

Why intoxicating liquors are so expensive

These remarks will partly illustrate why it is that for the enormous expenditure upon drink, such a small amount of labour is needed. In the case of the pig-stye, its cost represents—first, the value of the house destroyed to make way for it; and, secondly, the cost of its erection. In the case of the drink it represents the value of the grain, &c., destroyed for its manufacture, plus the cost of the labour expended in manufacturing it. The house was incomparably more useful than the stye; and if the three-and-a-half million loaves, represented in the grain destroyed, were used to feed the people, instead of being converted into drink, there is no sane person who will not admit, that such an appropriation would be infinitely more useful than when converted into drink. In one case it feeds the people, in the other it leads to their ruin.

The objection may perhaps again be started that I am arguing upon an extreme case, and that if people would only use these drinks in moderation, the argument would not apply.

I am free to admit that if the population of the Bury Union, instead of spending £375,000 per annum on drink, only spent say £20,000, the evil would be so far reduced; and, to say the least, the argument would proportionately lose its force. The argument, however, has to do with things as they are; and if ever such a happy change as I have indicated is to take place, it can only be brought about by exhibiting to the world the folly and madness of their present conduct.

The purpose of all labour is, or ought to be, to secure the physical comforts of life—good health, good food, warm clothing, and comfortable habitations; for although the end of man's existence is not to attend merely to the physical or animal, but primarily to the intellectual and spiritual, yet, inasmuch as the proper development of these faculties, depends upon the healthy condition of the physical organism, it is requisite, if we would fully develope the mental, to attend to the physical.

These remarks may perhaps, to some extent, appear to the reader wide of the question under discussion, and yet they are closely allied to it; because, if a man seeks sensual indulgence as the great end of his existence, reason is lost upon such a one, until he can be shown his folly. It is the mission of true political economy to show him this, and to elucidate the laws which conduce to individual happiness, and to the welfare of society generally.

I will now endeavour to apply the principles I have been trying to elucidate, to our expenditure nationally.

In a previous chapter it has been shown that the loss to the United Kingdom in intoxicating drinks is upwards of £200,000,000 per annum. If this money were spent as it ought to be, what would be the result?

How to expend £200,000,000 What the £200,000,000 annually lost through intoxicating drinks would do if properly expended:

Money Expended.		Persons Employed.
£25,000,000	Spent in manufactured goods, as clothing, bedding, &c., which would make up for what people are deficient, and would find employment for—say 400,000 persons, at an average of 14s. per week	400,000
£25,000,000		400,000

In manufactures.

£25,000,000		400,000	CHAP. VII.
£10,000,000	To be spent on food to supply those who do not now get enough; this would take about 30,000,000 bushels of the grain now wasted in the manufacture of drink		*In food.*
£30,000,000	To be spent in the erection of better houses, in making railways, building bridges, making better roads, and employing say 400,000 workmen, at 24s. each week	400,000	*In better dwellings, railways, &c.*
£20,000,000	To be laid out in the purchase of furniture for those whose houses are without these things through intemperance, and finding work for— say 250,000 persons at 24s. per week . . .	250,000	*In furniture.*
£20,000,000	To be spent in cultivating our waste land, and in improving the culture of those already occupied, and employing, say, 350,000 people at 17s. per week. . . .	350,000	*In cultivating waste land, &c.*
£105,000,000		1,400,000	

122 On the Right

CHAP. VII.

In sanitary improvements.

In building new schools.

In employing school teachers.

In establishing colleges.

In erecting places of worship.

	£105,000,000		1,400,000
	£20,000,000	To be spent in sanitary improvements, in applying the sewage from our towns to the land, and employing, say, 300,000 persons at 18s. per week	300,000
	£6,000,000	To be spent on building 5,000 new schools, in neglected districts, to cost £1,200 each, & finding work for, say, 80,000 men at 24s. per week .	80,000
	£2,400,000	To be paid to 10,000 additional school teachers, at £200 each per annum, and 20,000 pupil teachers at £20 per annum .	30,000
	£1,500,000	To be paid towards the higher branches of education (colleges, &c.) and employing 3,000 Professors at £500 per annum each	3,000
	£7,500,000	To be spent in erecting 5,000 places of worship in neglected districts, at £1,500 each, and employing 100,000 men at 24s. each per week . . .	100,000
	£142,400,000		1,913,000

£142,400,000		1,913,000	
£2,000,000	To be spent in maintaining 5,000 ministers to officiate therein, at £400 per annum	5,000	*In employing ministers.*
£3,000,000	To be paid to 30,000 individuals, to visit from house to house, to instruct the people, as to their moral, social, and domestic duties, at salaries of £100 each per annum	30,000	*In employing Home Missionaries.*
£5,000,000	To be paid to 10,000 Christian missionaries, to go forth to instruct and Christianize the heathen world, at a cost—say of £500 each per annum	10,000	*In sending Missionaries to the Heathen.*
£5,000,000	To be paid to establish 10,000 libraries in towns and villages where they have been neglected, at £500 each, and finding employment in printing, &c., for, say	50,000	*In founding libraries.*
£157,400,000		2,008,000	

CHAP. VII.	£157,400,000	2,008,000
In supporting young children and aged people.	£5,000,000 To be paid yearly to 30,000 fatherless children, aged and infirm and sick paupers, at an average cost each of from six to seven shillings per week . . .	300,000
In keeping children longer at school.	£2,250,000 To be paid for the lost wages of 300,000 young people, at 3s. per week, who are now employed, but whom it would be well to keep at school till they are thirteen years of age	300,000
In relaxation and enjoyment.	£10,000,000 Which would probably be spent in relaxation and enjoyment, such as seaside visits, &c., and employing, say 62,000 attendants, &c. . . .	62,000
In partial support to aged people	£2,000,000* To be spent in supporting 200,000 aged people, who would at an earlier period partially retire from labour, at 4s. each per week	200,000
	£176,650,000	2,870,000

* This expenditure would doubtless be provided for by the people, in their younger years, laying by a store for old age, so that they might partly labour, and partly live upon previous earnings.

£176,650,000	2,870,000
£15,000,000* To be paid for making up the loss to the revenue which would arise from the giving up of intoxicating drinks, leaving	
£8,350,000 £4,350,000 for sundries	
£200,000,000	2,870,000

In these calculations, the reader will see, that all the money does not go in the shape of wages; a considerable sum is allowed for the purchase of material from other countries; but then, as a rule, these countries would, in return, take the product of our manufactures. We should therefore gain in this respect as much as we should lose, so that we might in reality take the whole of the £200,000,000 as expended in labour. If we did so we might add another 1½ million workers to the list we have given, or say a total of 5,000,000 persons employed, or supported, which would represent a population of 10,000,000 people, or one-third of the entire population of the United Kingdom.

These estimates may be increased.

* The question is sometimes asked, If people give up drinking, What is to become of the revenue? The problem to solve is,—given a saving of £200,000,000 wherewith to pay £25,000,000. Any schoolboy would be able to see that one year's cost of drink, will pay the revenue derived therefrom for eight years, even granting that the whole £25,000,000 would be lost to the revenue. Such, however, would not be the case. It would be lost to the excise department, but it would, to a great extent, be made up by the increase in the income and property taxes. It would also be made up in another way, by a reduction in the National expenditure, for a sober people, would not tolerate the lavish expenditure which has characterized our exchequer.

I will, however, assume that only 3,000,000 persons are thus employed. These would represent 6,000,000 of a population, who would be supported if the £200,000,000 which it now costs this country through intoxicating liquors, were properly expended.

Let us look at the other side.

Persons employed by money spent in drink.

As we have seen, there are 98,009 publicans and 52,590 beer sellers, or a total of 150,599 persons who are employed in selling liquors, besides a number of others on a smaller scale. If we add these together, and also include those who are engaged in malting, brewing, &c., we shall probably have—say 100,000 more, or 250,000 in all. If we add another 150,000 as servants, we shall, taking an extreme estimate, raise the total of persons employed in one way or another—say to 400,000, which would represent a population of 800,000.

A contrast.

Let us contrast the result arising from these two expenditures. In one case the £200,000,000 would give employment to 3,000,000 people; in the other to 400,000.*

---

* It has been said, in objection to the argument in reference to the small number of men employed in the liquor manufacture, that, in a bad business, the fewer the men employed the better. Everything else being the same, this would be logical,—that is, if man for man, the same evil resulted when 200,000 men are employed as when 100,000 are employed, then there would be, as a consequence, double the evil; but, if, from the labour of the 200,000 there only resulted the same evil as from the 100,000, then the argument falls to the ground, whilst the employment of 100,000 men extra would be a good, inasmuch as it would decrease the list of the unemployed. It would simply be appropriating so much more of the money in payment for labour, instead of paying for grain destroyed, &c.! This, whilst it would not increase the evil of intem-

The entire manual labour, or industrial classes, in the United Kingdom amount to about 12,000,000 of our population, of whom 400,000, as we have seen, are directly or indirectly employed by the liquor traffic. Supposing this to be correct, the two cases will stand thus :

No. of manual labour classes.

The income of the United Kingdom, when expended in such a manner as to include the present drink bill, will give employment to 12,000,000 people, of whom 400,000 are engaged in destructive labour.

If this income were properly invested, so as to exclude the expenditure upon intoxicating liquors, it would give employment to 15,000,000 persons, who would be engaged, not in destructive, but in productive labour.

In the case where the drink bill forms part of our expenditure, we employ nearly 3,000,000 fewer labourers, whilst of those who are employed, 400,000 are engaged in destroying what is produced by the other 12,000,000; for they destroy such a quantity of grain yearly as would make bread equal to 1,000,000,000 4lb. loaves.

But it is not in loss of work, or in distruction of grain merely, that we suffer through intemperance. There are other evils even more terrible than these, The loss of material wealth is deplorable, especially

Moral evils resulting from intemperance.

---

perance, would decrease the number of paupers to the extent of the additional number of men who might be so employed. It would therefore work good in two ways, 1st, in saving the grain, and 2nd, in finding more work for our unemployed population.

when it floods a country with destitution and suffering; but the loss of intelligence, and virtue, and morality, is infinitely more deplorable. The use of intoxicating liquors is the most prolific cause of moral degradation, ignorance, intemperance, crime, lunacy, loss of life, and, indeed, of all the social evils which so appal the heart of the philanthropic statesman, or of the Christian worker.

To tabulate a few of its evil results. It may be asserted that—

Criminals. It is the cause of 100,000 out of the 140,000 criminals who are constantly incarcerated in our gaols.

Thieves, &c. It supplies society with a great proportion of the 54,249 known thieves, depredators, receivers of stolen goods, &c., and possibly with as many more that are unknown.

Vagrants. It also supplies a vagrant and vagabond population of at least 250,000.

Drunkards Assuming that on an average there are four habitual, or occasional drunkards connected with each public-house, it gives us a total of 600,000 drunkards; all of whom render their homes unhappy, whilst many of them entail upon their families—embracing innocent and helpless children—the most dreadful miseries.

Policemen. It necessitates the employment of 20,000 out of the 25,000 policemen required to preserve the peace.

It leads to most of the accidents and crimes which occasion the 25,000 inquests which are held annually, and it cuts short the lives of multitudes of others, many of them innocent children, so as to involve the untimely deaths of at least 50,000 or 60,000 persons yearly.

Inquests and untimely deaths.

This picture is one that it is sad to contemplate, and yet it gives but an imperfect idea of the demoralization and misery constantly created in this country through drinking; and yet, we pride ourselves upon being the most enlightened and religious people in the world. What our country might become were it not for drink it is impossible to forecast; but, to quote the language of a distinguished living statesman, "it would be so changed, and so changed for the better, that it would be almost impossible to know it again."*

What the banishment of drink would do.

The Right Hon. John Bright's opinion.

If we consider the subject in relation to its influence upon the future, its importance cannot be over-rated. Let the reader imagine the contrast in twenty years time, between 3,000,000 of people

---

* "If we could subtract from the ignorance, the poverty, the suffering, the sickness, and the crime which are now witnessed amongst us, the ignorance, the poverty, the suffering, the sickness, and the crime which are caused by one single, but the most prevalent, habit or vice of drinking needlessly, which destroys the body, and mind, and home, and family; do we not all feel that this country would be so changed, and so changed for the better, that it would be almost impossible for us to know it again? Let me, then, in conclusion, say what it is upon my heart to say, what I know to be true, what I have felt every hour of my life when I have been discussing great questions affecting the condition of the working classes,—let me say this to all the people, that it is by the combination of a wise government and a virtuous people, and not otherwise—mark that—that we may hope to make some steps to that blessed time when there shall be 'no complaining in our streets,' and when 'our garners may be full, affording all manner of store.'"—Speech of the Right Hon. John Bright, at Birmingham, January, 1870.

I

CHAP. VII.
The influence of these in the future contrasted.

being employed in productive labour, filling the land with wealth, comfort, and happiness, and 400,000 engaged in destructive labour, destroying not only the food and other material wealth created by the industry of others, but also destroying the people themselves, both physically and morally. In one case there would be a perpetual and rapid accumulation of material, moral and intellectual, as well as physical wealth to such an extent as to increase enormously our entire national property; and what would be of far more importance than this, we should be rid of most of the evils we so much deplore, and in their place would be substituted virtue, intelligence, and all the other social blessings that are so much to be desired.

CHAPTER VIII.

THE REMEDY.

NOTWITHSTANDING the enormous wealth we possess, and the exceptional facilities we enjoy for increasing that wealth, it is a sorrowful but undeniable fact, that about one out of every ten of our entire population, or one-fifth of the industrial classes of our country, become, during the course of a year, chargeable to the community as paupers, there are many others, who, whilst they do not become chargeable to the public, become chargeable to their relatives and friends, whilst others, too high minded to trouble either their friends or the public, struggle on in poverty and suffering, unaided by others, and unable to help themselves, simply for the reason that they cannot get employment whereby to earn the means of subsistence.

Such a state of things is most deplorable, and has naturally caused the deepest concern in the minds of our philanthropists and statesmen.

During the last three or four years, many meetings and conferences have been held for the purpose of devising some plan, whereby their evils might be mitigated. So great had the destitution become, especially in the east end of London, that

Lamentable destitution of our population.

Remedial action contemplated.

on the 17th of June, 1870, Mr. Torrens, Member for Finsbury, brought the question before the House of Commons, by moving the following resolution:—

Mr. Torren's resolution in Parliament.

"That the continued want of employment amongst those who lived by waged labour, in many of the great towns of the kingdom calls for the special consideration of this House, with a view to the means that may best be devised for the remedy of the same without delay."

Mr. Torrens, in addressing the House, went on to urge, that "means should be devised to facilitate the emigration of those who were now destitute by no fault of their own, but solely because there was no employment for them."

Emigration recommended.

At most of the meetings or conferences which have been held, emigration has generally been suggested as the remedy whereby these evils are to be rectified.

In what way is it thought that emigration will prove a remedy for the evils referred to?

The idea generally entertained, and the wish of intelligent persons who advocate it, is that emigrants who leave our shores should go to Australia or some other colony or country, where land is plentiful and cheap, and grow corn or cotton to be shipped to us, and, in return for these products, take back our manufactures.

Object of emigration.

There would be some plausibility in advocating emigration of this kind, if the intended emigrants who were out of employment, were Dorsetshire or

Wiltshire labourers, who, when engaged in work, earn only their 8s. per week; but when the persons out of employment are our skilled artisans, the remedy is altogether inapplicable.

Emigrants should be agricultural labourers.

It should be borne in mind that the artisan population of our large towns, and in the country generally, are entirely ignorant of agriculture. What are these to do, when they get out in the back settlements of our colonies? Ignorant of farm duties, and isolated from any society where they could secure instruction or help, they would be totally incapable of making their way. It would be as reasonable to send the agricultural labourers of Dorsetshire to establish some colonial manufactory, as it would be to send the artisan population of our large towns, to break up and cultivate the unoccupied lands of our colonies. If, therefore, our artisans emigrate they must emigrate as artisans, and not as farmers, and seek employment at their own trades in the countries to which they go. What would be the influence of this?

Artisans are totally unfitted to emigrate.

Except as artisans.

1st. It would take from our country a portion of our skilled population—those who produce the wealth—and transport them with their skill and energy, and wealth-creating powers, to labour for other countries.

Artisans are wealth producers.

2nd. It would establish in other lands, manufactories superintended by workmen who have been trained by ourselves, and who possess all the skill that we do, but who, when they emigrate, are relieved from the heavy taxation which presses upon

He would take his skill to compete with us in other lands

us, and are therefore placed, in this respect, in more favourable circumstances than ourselves for competing in the markets of the world.

These people, therefore, if sent into other countries would become competitors of ours, and rob us of our trade.

3rd. The fact, too, should not be forgotten, that when our artisans are sent away they not only cease to create wealth for us, but they also cease to pay taxes; their share of the country's burdens, therefore, falls upon those who are left behind, upon whom taxation must fall in a correspondingly increased degree. And though, perhaps, if it were a matter of necessity, it would be better for us to let them go, and pay their share of the country's taxation, rather than pay the taxes and keep the men as well; yet, inasmuch as the destitution is the result of our misconduct, the proper way to act is, to correct our own folly, and then there would be full employment for them at home.

If, as has been shown in the previous chapters, the industrial classes of our country are those who create the country's wealth, it must follow, as a consequence, that in proportion as these are sent out of the country so will decrease its wealth-producing powers.

But, then, it is said: What must be done! Our people are starving for want of employment, and we must either support them at home or ship them to countries where they can support themselves.

If emigration would, in this respect, do everything that its most sanguine advocates desire, it is a remedy which should be adopted only as a last resource. If however, as I have shown, emigration under present circumstances would fail to remedy the evil, and would moreover be prejudicial to the interests of the country, its adoption becomes entirely out of the question.

The attention of our rulers, and of our philanthropists should be directed, not to searching for some foreign country where our people may be shipped off to find employment, and earn a comfortable and honest living; but to trying to make our own land such, as that the industry of the honest artisan may meet with its reward.

In what way is this desirable result to be obtained?

It has been clearly shown in the foregoing chapters, that the enormous amount of money which is expended upon intoxicating liquors by the people of this country, is the main cause of pauperism and destitution, and that if this money were properly applied it would give employment to 3,000,000 more people than are now employed, and, therefore, the cause of our destitution, as well as the remedy for the same, lies within ourselves.

The problem therefore to solve is, not, how shall our artisans and our labouring classes be transported into other countries, so that employment may be found them, and they may escape from the demoralization and destitution which befalls them in

CHAP. VIII.

The remedy illustrated.

this country, but, how shall the influences which demoralize and impoverish them here be removed.

If in the city of Manchester, in consequence of imperfect drainage or sewage, or from any other cause, the people were subjected to fever and pestilence, the duty of the authorities would be, not to send the citizens away, but to investigate the causes of the fever, and remove them as speedily as possible.

So, in reference to the pauperism and the other evils of the country, it is the business of those who are in authority, not to transport the people to other lands, away from the causes which impoverish them, but to investigate the causes which reduce our people to poverty; for if they emigrate, and the causes which have impoverished those who thus emigrate, be permitted to continue to operate, those who are left behind will, by and bye, fall victims to the same influences.

The question, therefore, to be settled is, How shall these habits of intemperance be corrected? The answer is, by removing the causes which occasion them. What are those causes?

Universal condemnation of drunkenness.

Whatever may be the opinion of individuals in reference to the question of total abstinence, there is but one opinion as to drunkenness. All alike condemn it as being hurtful to the health, to the pocket, to the character, and to the happiness not only of the individual, who may be addicted to it, but to all who may in any way be connected with him; and yet, notwithstanding this universal condemnation of drunkenness, it is estimated that there are not less than 600,000 habitual drunkards in the United Kingdom all of whom (or with very few exceptions) acknowledge, and mourn their folly, and repeatedly vow that they will cease to act the drunkard's part, and become wiser and better men.

How comes it, that these good resolves are so seldom carried into effect? How is it that, despite their convictions, despite their resolves, despite the admonition of friends, and the entreaties of their families, such vast numbers of our population go on in habits that involve them in misery, and lead them to ruin? To ask the question is to answer it; every one knows that it is owing to the numerous and powerful temptations of the public-house and the beershops which beset their path.

It has been shown in a previous chapter, that in the United Kingdom, to a population of 30,838,210 persons, there are 150,599 public-houses and beer-shops, being one to every 40 houses, or to every 204 of the population; in addition to which there are 35,497 wine sellers, spirit dealers, &c.

The point I wish the reader to note in reference to these figures is, the enormous number of the houses in proportion to the population.

Why is it that such an enormous number of persons are licensed to sell intoxicating drinks? Is it in order to provide a ready and sure way for the destruction of wealth? Is it in order that the people may become drunken and degraded? There is no one, no matter how zealously he might advocate the granting of licenses, who would not repel with scorn such an insinuation; but then there is such an enormous number, that it is impossible for them to exist, except by the intemperance of the people; and, therefore, to what else does such a wholesale establishment of public-houses amount to?

I know that those who advocate the granting of licences, generally do so under the plea of "meeting the requirements of the neighbourhood"—"providing the working man with his beer, &c." Originally, on the first establishment of public-houses, such a plea might have been a justification; but when the sad experience of hundreds of years has established the fact that so sure as a public-house is licensed, so sure is there drunkenness and all its attendant evils; under such circumstances, the licensing of a house is equivalent to licensing the resulting evils, and those who do it incur the guilt, and are responsible for the consequences.

The licensing system, as it at present exists, has been prostituted, until it has become nothing more than a huge legalised machinery whereby wealthy Brewers, Distillers, and Publicans may, not, supply the supposed wants of the public, but, sell as much of their beer as possible. It is an arrangement whereby these men are enabled to destroy the food of the people, filch from them their earnings, convert them into besotted drunkards, and very frequently also into paupers and criminals, who ultimately have to be maintained or punished at the expense of the ratepayers. Surely! an enlightened nation will cease to tolerate this.

It is the testimony of universal experience, that in proportion as facilities for the sale of intoxicating drinks are multiplied, so will be the increase of drunkenness. I might fill volumes with evidence to prove this, but I will only refer to a report of the Committee of the Convocation* of the Province of Canterbury,† recently issued.

On the 14th of June, 1869, a committee of the Lower House of Convocation for the Province of Canterbury issued a voluminous report, which was printed by order of the House, containing the results of most extensive inquiries from the Clergy of the Provinces, and also from Recorders, Governors

Marginal notes: CHAP. VIII. Drinking in proportion to the facilities provided. Report of the committee of the Convocation of the Province of Canterbury.

---

* The Province of Canterbury comprises the following 32 English counties, and North and South Wales, with a population of 14,071,164:—Bedfordshire, Berkshire, Buckinghamshire, Cambridgeshire, Cornwall, Derbyshire, Devonshire, Dorsetshire, Essex, Gloucestershire, Hampshire, Herefordshire, Hertfordshire, Huntingdonshire, Kent, Leicestershire, Lincolnshire, Middlesex, Norfolk, Northamptonshire, Nottinghamshire, Oxfordshire, Rutland, Shropshire, Somerset, Staffordshire, Suffolk, Surrey, Sussex, Warwickshire, Wiltshire, and Worcestershire.

† The following were the Members of the Committee:—

The Prolocutor	Canon Argles,
Dean of Canterbury,	„ Carus,
„ Chichester,	„ Gillett,
„ Westminster.	„ Harvey,
Archdeacon of Coventry,	„ Oxenden,
„ Ely,	„ Wood,
„ Exeter,	„ Dr. Fraser,
„ Leicester,	Prebendary Gibbs,
„ Nottingham,	„ Kemp.
„ Salop.	Archdeacon of Coventry, Chairman.

and Chaplains of Gaols, Chief Constables, Superintendents of Police, Coroners, Governors of Workhouses, Lunatic Asylums, &c., throughout England, asking their opinions as to the causes of, and the remedies for, intemperance. In their report they say—" It also appears an unquestionable fact that, in proportion as facilities in any shape for procuring intoxicating liquors are countenanced and afforded, the vice of intemperance, and its dismal effects, are everywhere increased. This conclusion, the evidence before your committee amply confirms."

Number of returns published.

In corroboration of this statement, the committee have published 2,283 returns, received from all parts of the country, the facts of which fully confirm the conclusions of the report; and I would urge the reader, if he does not agree with the conclusion of the committee, to get the said report, and examine the evidence upon which its conclusions are based. If he does, all his doubts will be dispelled.

Suggestions of the committee.

In their report the Committee suggest a number of remedies for the removal of intemperance. Amongst others are the following:—

Repeal of the Beer Act.

1. The repeal of the Beer Act of 1830, and the total suppression of beerhouses throughout the country.

Closing public houses on Sundays.

2. The closing of public-houses on the Lord's Day, except for the accommodation of *bona fide* travellers.

4. A great reduction in the number of public-houses throughout the kingdom, it being in

evidence that the number already licensed far exceeds the real demand, and that in proportion as facilities for drinking are reduced, intemperance, with its manifold evils, is restrained.

Chap. VIII.
Reduction in the number.

6. The rigid enforcement of the penalties now attached to drunkenness, both on the actual offenders and on licensed persons who allow drunkenness to occur on their premises.

Enforcement of the law as to drunkenness, &c.

The eleventh recommendation, which is the last, is a very important one, it is as follows:—

11. Your Committee, in conclusion, are of opinion that as the ancient and avowed object of licensing the sale of intoxicating liquors is to supply a supposed public want, without detriment to the public welfare, a legal power of restraining the issue or renewal of licenses should be placed in the hands of the persons most deeply interested and affected, namely, the inhabitants themselves—who are entitled to protection from the injurious consequences of the present system. Such a power would, in effect, secure to the districts, willing to exercise it, the advantages now enjoyed by the numerous parishes in the province of Canterbury, where, according to reports furnished to your committee, owing to the influence of the landowner, no sale of intoxicating liquors is licensed.

The inhabitants to have a power of veto.

The report concludes as follows:—" Few, it

may be believed, are cognizant of the fact—which has been elicited by the present inquiry—that there are at this time, within the province of Canterbury, upwards of one thousand parishes in which there is neither public-house nor beershop; and where, in consequence of the absence of these inducements to crime and pauperism, according to the evidence before the committee, the intelligence, morality, and comfort of the people are such as the friends of temperance would have anticipated."

Results following the absence of public houses in 1000 parishes.

The five recommendations given above comprise the reforms which are needed in order to banish the evils of intemperance. The duty of the Legislature, therefore, is—

Duty of the Legislature

1. To repeal the Beer Act of 1830, and abolish beerhouses throughout the country.
2. Close all public-houses on the Lord's Day.
3. Reduce the number, to such a proportion of the population, say one public-house to 2,500 inhabitants—so that it shall not be necessary, as it is at present, in order that public-houses pay, that there shall be a drunken population.
4. Rigidly enforce the penalties now attached to drunkenness, &c., both against the buyer and the seller, and then
5. As the Convocation Report says, "It being the ancient and avowed object of the licensing the sale of intoxicating liquors, to supply a supposed public want, without detriment to the public welfare," let the inhabitants

in each parish or township, where they think it may promote the public weal, be empowered to prevent altogether the issue of licenses for the sale of intoxicating liquors in their locality.

I am aware that there are individuals who object to the closing of public-houses,* as being an interference with the rights of the publican and the liberty of the subject. There are two classes of rights, moral rights and legal rights; the former are common to all, the latter are granted by the law to serve the interests of the community. If the publican has a moral right to sell, so has every citizen of the state. If it be a right created by law in order to restrain an evil, the whole argument is granted; for the restraint may be, and ought to be, exercised to the extent needed to deal with the evil, otherwise it ought not to be applied at all.

Perhaps it will be said, that in such a case there must be a choice of evils; that though the existence of public-houses may be an evil, yet to close them altogether would be a greater evil: suppose this were granted, who is to judge as to the measure of the evil? It is professedly for the people's good that these places are established, and, therefore, they ought to be the judges. There

---

* In speaking of the closing of public-houses, the reader will please bear in mind, that the reference is only to closing them as places for the sale of intoxicating liquors. They might still continue to be public-houses in the proper sense of the term—that is, victualling houses, instead of tippling houses.

CHAP. VIII.

The people should therefore decide.

is never an evil but there are parties interested in its perpetuation. If a portion only of the community are made into the judges, they might be swayed by interest, as is now too commonly the case; but when the people decide, conflicting interests check one another; besides, in a free country why should one class presume to decide for another; let the people decide by a direct vote. If they believe public-houses to be more of good than harm, then they will allow them to go on; but, if they believe them to do more harm than good, they will then vote for their being closed altogether, a more equitable plan could not be devised.

It is argued by some, that the proper remedy for the evils of intemperance is, to reduce the number of public-houses to such proportion, and apply such a strict supervision over them as to strip them of their evil influences; and yet, that those who wish to obtain their glass of beer, may not have their liberty in this respect interfered with.

For 400 years, our legislators have been trying to accomplish this result, but to day the evils are as many, and as lamentable, if not more so, than ever.

It must not be overlooked by those who argue thus, that it is a very easy matter for people who wish, to brew their own beer at home, and therefore, if public-houses were closed, they might get what they desired—at half the price, freer from adulteration, and away from the temptations and dangers incident to the public-house.

CHAP. VIII.

The problem, for those who plead for public-houses to solve, is, given—a seductive liquor, a publican interested in pushing its sale, and the temptation of company to aid him. How shall these powerful influences for evil be concentrated in a public-house, and society be saved from the resulting evils.

But even, if by vigilant oversight, public-houses might be so kept in bounds, as that there would be few, if any, resulting evils, the ratepayers even then might very properly ask themselves the question, is the slight supposed convenience which is obtained from licensing these houses, worth the amount of labour, cost, and danger incurred to keep them right? if not, then to continue their existence is to choose the greater of two evils, which is opposed to every principle, both of common sense, and right, and therefore they ought to be prohibited.

There are individuals who hold the opinion that the spread of education will ultimately be effectual in removing the evil of intemperance. This opinion, however, is entirely opposed to the experience of mankind in all ages, and in all countries. Education will, doubtless, have its influence; but that influence must be to teach people to respect themselves, and to avoid the cause of intemperance; otherwise it will be ineffectual. But, if education could be shown to be a perfect cure, why should a

Education as a remedy

K

CHAP. VIII.

Folly of creating evils against which we have to labour.

State license a system so fraught with evil, and then have to waste its energies in educating the people to contend against it. At the present time four-fifths of the educational moral power of the country is lost in contending against evils that are self-created. Why should it be so? If it could be shown that in the end we should be successful, though this in the nature of things is impossible, for it is not possible for a nation to be so vicious as to flood the land with besetments to evil, and yet be virtuous enough to withstand them. The virtue that will withstand the evils will put them away; but if it could be shown that education under such circumstances would be successful, why should we create these antagonistic influences to paralyze and stultify our labours for good. To quote again the words of Mr. Gladstone, "Government ought to make it easy to do right and difficult to do wrong."

Mission of Government.-

At present it is the opposite of this, for it lends its authority and co-operation to a system whose influence is to beset every effort for good, to rob the people of their hard earnings, to waste the nation's wealth, and to bring demoralization, misery, and ruin upon the people themselves.

APPENDIX.

APPENDIX A.

The returns of malt and sugar used in the following calculations will be found upon the last page but one of the Trade and Navigation Returns for December 31st in each year. The returns of British spirits will be found upon the same page. The quantity of wine and foreign and colonial spirits for each year are taken from the Statistical Abstract for 1870, page 71. The British wines, cider, perry, &c., are estimated, as they are not given in any return.

TABLES OF THE QUANTITIES AND COST OF INTOXICATING LIQUORS USED DURING EACH OF THE FOUR YEARS ENDING 1861.

1858.

	Gallons.	£
British Spirits.........	23,212,612 @ 20/-	23,212,612
Foreign and Colonial Spirits.............	4,582,313 ,, 24/-	5,498,775
Wine	6,268,685 ,, 21/-	6,582,119
Beer (Malt), 40,375,115 bush...	726,752,070 ,, 1/6	54,506,405
British Wines, Cider, Perry, &c.	12,500,000 ,, 2/-	1,250,000
	773,315,680 gallons	£91,049,911

1859.

	Gallons.	£
British Spirits.........	23,878,688 @ 20/-	23,878,688
Foreign and Colonial Spirits...............	4,932,648 ,, 24/-	5,919,177
Wine	6,775,992 ,, 21/-	7,114,791
Beer (Malt), 42,759,065 bush...	769,663,170 ,, 1/6	57,724,737
British Wines, Cider, Perry, &c.	12,500,000 ,, 2/-	1,250,000
	817,750,498 gallons	£95,887,393

1860.

	Gallons.	£
British Spirits.........	21,404,088 @ 20/-	21,404,088
Foreign and Colonial Spirits...............	5,521,923 ,, 24/-	6,626,307
Wine	6,718,585 ,, 21/-	7,054,514
Beer (Malt), 37,453,907 bush...	674,170,326 ,, 1/6	50,562,774
British Wines, Cider, Perry, &c.	12,500,000 ,, 2/-	1,250,000
	720,314,922 gallons.	£86,897,683

1861.

	Gallons.	£
British Spirits.........	19,698,792 @ 20/-	19,698,792
Foreign and Colonial Spirits...............	5,193,070 ,, 24/-	6,231,684
Wine	10,693,071 ,, 18/-*	9,623,763
Beer (Malt), 43,065,088 bush...	775,171,584 ,, 1/6	58,137,868
British Wines, Cider, Perry, &c.	12,500,000 ,, 2/-	1,250,000
	823,256,517 gallons.	£94,942,107

* In 1860 the duty on wine was reduced about 3s. 2d. per gallon on the average.

SUMMARY.

	Quantity used.	Cost.
	Gallons.	£
1858	773,315,680	91,019,911
1859	817,750,498	95,887,393
1860	720,314,922	86,897,683
1861	823,256,517	94,912,107
	3,134,637,617	£368,777,094
Annual average	783,659,404	£92,194,273

APPENDIX B.

TABLES OF THE QUANTITIES AND COST OF INTOXICATING LIQUORS USED IN THE UNITED KINGDOM DURING EACH OF THE FOUR YEARS ENDING 1869.

1866.

	Gallons.		£
British Spirits	22,516,336	@ 20/-	22,516,336
Foreign and Colonial Spirits	7,797,470	„ 24/-	9,356,964
Wine	13,244,864	„ 18/-	11,920,377
Beer			
Sugar used in brewing 145,437 cwt., equivalent to 620,528¾ bus. — Bushels. 50,838,356⅔	915,090,415	„ 1/6	68,631,781
Malt used in brewing 50,217,828 b.			
British Wines, Cider, Perry, &c.	15,000,000	„ 2/-	1,500,000
	973,649,085 galls.		£113,925,458

Appendix.

1867.

		Gallons.	£
British Spirits		21,589,969 @ 20/-	21,589,969
Foreign and Colonial Spirits		8,339,155 ,, 24/-	10,006,986
Wine		13,673,793 ,, 18/-	12,306,413
Beer			
Sugar used in brewing 381,930 cwt., equivalent to 1,629,568 bs. Malt used in brewing 46,310,357 b.	Bushels. 47,939,925	862,918,650 ,, 1/6	64,718,898
British Wines, Cider, Perry, &c.		15,000,000 ,, 2/-	1,500,000
		921,521,567 galls.	£110,122,266

1868.

		Gallons.	£
British Spirits		21,341,449 @ 20/-	21,341,449
Foreign and Colonial Spirits		8,398,817 ,, 24/-	10,078,580
Wine		15,064,575 ,, 18/-	13,558,117
Beer			
Sugar used in brewing 351,742 cwt. equivalent to 1,500,765$\frac{13}{15}$ bs. Malt used in brewing 48,119,033 b	Bushels. 49,619,798$\frac{13}{15}$	893,156,379$\frac{3}{5}$ @ 1/6	66,986,728
British Wines, Cider, Perry, &c.		15,000,000 ,, 2/-	1,500,000
		952,961,220$\frac{3}{5}$ galls.	£113,464,874

1869.

	Gallons.	£
British Spirits	21,941,779 @ 20/-	21,941,779
Foreign and Colonial Spirits	8,172,845 ,, 24/-	9,807,414
Wine	14,734,534 ,, 18/-	13,261,080
Beer — Sugar used in brewing 342,678 cwt., equivalent to 1,462,092¼ b. Malt used in brewing 47,704,819 b.	Bushels. 49,166,911¼ = 885,004,412⅔ @ 1/6	66,375,330
British Wines, Cider, Perry, &c.	15,000,000 ,, 2/-	1,500,000
	944,853,570⅔ galls.	£112,885,603

SUMMARY.

	Quantity used.	Cost.
	Gallons.	£
1866	973,649,085	113,925,458
1867	921,521,567	110,122,266
1868	952,961,220¾	113,464,874
1869	944,853,570⅔	112,885,603
	3,792,985,443 galls.	£450,398,201
Annual Average	948,246,360	£112,599,550

The items which form the basis of the preceding calculations, as to the quantity and cost of intoxicating liquors consumed in the United Kingdom, are taken from returns issued by Government.

In the case of beer, the returns are not given as beer, but as malt and sugar from which the quantity of beer has to be calculated. The Excise estimate is, that 2 bushels of malt will make 1 barrel or 36 gallons of beer, and that 210lbs. of sugar will make as much beer as 8 bushels of malt; and therefore in the preceding calculations the sugar has been converted into its equivalent in malt, and added to the malt. The calculation then becomes simply a matter of proportion, thus :—If 2 bushels of malt will give 36 gallons of beer, what will the total number of bushels give? During the four years ending 1861, a comparatively small annual amount of sugar was used in brewing, but in each of the four years ending 1869 it was extensively used. To make clear these remarks, I will take the figures for the year 1869 as an illustration. That year there was 342,678 cwt. of sugar and 47,704,819 bushels of malt used in brewing. If the 342,678 cwt. of sugar be reduced into lbs., and then divided by 210 and multiplied by 8, it will give 1,462,092$\frac{4}{5}$ bushels, the number of bushels which 342,678 cwt. of sugar is equivalent to. Adding this to the 47,704,819 bushels of malt, it gives 49,166,911$\frac{4}{5}$ bushels. If this be multiplied by 36 (the number of gallons in a barrel) and divided by 2 (the number of bushels of malt which will make a barrel of beer), it gives the total number of gallons of beer which these bushels will make, amounting to 885,004,412$\frac{2}{5}$. At 4$\frac{1}{2}$d. per quart (my estimate of the average retail selling price), it gives £66,375,330 as expended upon beer alone in 1869.

The reader will bear in mind that the preceding tables are all based upon the supposition that intoxicating drinks are all free from adulteration or dilution, and that there is never any illicit manufacturing takes place. They assume that all the beer is made from malt and hops or sugar, and that all the wine is the juice of the grape, and that the spirits are the product of distillation. It is, however, a notorious fact, that beer is very much adulterated,* and that the adulteration of wines and spirits is

---

* Mr. Phillips, principal of the Laboratory of the Analytical Department for the Inland Revenue, reports as follows :—" During the last financial year 26 samples of beer and materials found in the possession of licensed brewers have been analysed, and of these 20 were found to be illicit; the prohibited ingredients being, in 14 samples, grains of paradise ; one of these samples containing, in addition, tobacco : in two others cocculus indicus was present in large and dangerous quantities ; two samples contained capsicum ; and the remaining two proto-sulphate of iron. Generally

carried on to as great extent as that of beer. If, therefore, a fair allowance were made for this adulteration, it would very much increase the amount of the estimates I have given.

The estimates here given as to the cost of intoxicating liquors used, are higher than those given in the author's pamphlet on the "Depression in the Cotton Trade;" but having given a much fuller examination to the subject since the publication of that pamphlet, the author is convinced that the calculations there given are below the mark. On this point there may be differences of opinion, but whether the same be more or less does not affect the argument at all.

In the "British Almanack" for 1870 there is an article on self-imposed taxation, by Samuel Smiles, in which he gives the expenditure upon intoxicating drinks in the United Kingdom during 1868 as follows:—

	Gallons.	£
Home and Foreign Spirits	29,418,535	30,568,232
Beer	749,983,824	43,749,056
Wines	15,151,741	12,987,927
Cider, Perry, and British Wines, say		1,500,000
		£88,805,215

the prohibited materials employed in the adulteration of beer are not injurious to health, the object of the fraudulent brewers or retailers of beer being more to increase the bulk of their goods than to render the beer stupifying by the addition of noxious materials. Still, he says, there can be little doubt that the practice of adulterating beer with poisonous matters, such as tobacco and cocculus indicus, is more prevalent than might be inferred from the small number of detections made, as the fraud is difficult to discover unless the offender be caught in the act of committing it. Considering, therefore, this circumstance, and the abominable character of the offence, Mr. Phillips is of opinion that it would be only just to the community to make public the names of those persons convicted of adding cocculus indicus or other deleterious substances to beer brewed for sale; and he feels no hesitation in stating that the two instances of the use of the dangerous drug in question occurred in the neighbourhood of Wirksworth, in Derbyshire, and that many of the detections of the use of grains of paradise were also made in the same district. He states also that the experience of many years had led him to the conclusion that the adulteration of beer with drugs, as distinguished from the mere dilution or increasing of the bulk of the article, is more prevalent in the Midland counties and the West Riding of Yorkshire than in any other part of the kingdom."—*Report of Inland Revenue for 1864, Appendix, page 19.*

The above estimate is upwards of £24,000,000 less than the one I give. From whence arises the difference, and which estimate is correct?

In the items of spirits and wines there is very little difference between the calculations of Mr. Smiles and my own. In spirits the quantity Mr. Smiles gives is less than in the table I have given. The difference probably arises from the fact, that he gives his figures from the Inland Revenue Returns, which are made up to March 31st, while mine are given from the Trade and Navigation Returns, which are made up to the 31st of December.

The main discrepancy is in the item of beer. Mr. Smiles estimates $3\frac{1}{4}$ barrels of beer to 8 bushels of malt, whereas I take the Excise estimate of 4 barrels to 8 bushels. Mr. Smiles estimates the beer at $3\frac{1}{2}$d. per quart; my estimate is $4\frac{1}{2}$d. He himself, speaking of his estimate, says, "It will probably be admitted that this estimate is very considerably within the probable expenditure." The selling price of beer ranges from 4d. to 8d. per quart,* and therefore $4\frac{1}{2}$d. appears to me to be a very moderate estimate, especially if we take into consideration the fact, that no allowance is made for adulteration. I think 5d. would be about the average selling price, but I have taken $4\frac{1}{2}$d. in order to be within the mark.

* It is said to be customary for some of the London publicans to sell beer at 3d. and 3½d. per quart. They are enabled to do this by the extensive dilution they practise. In the Appendix to the Report of the Commissioners of Inland Revenue for 1865, Mr. Phillips, the principal of the Laboratory, remarks:—"Thus, the most usual mode of adulterating beer, and one which there are good grounds for believing is very generally practised by the publicans of London, is to add water to the beverage, the injury to the fullness or 'body' of the article arising from this dilution being repaid by the introduction of sugar, treacle, &c."

APPENDIX C.

The reader who has read the pamphlet published by the writer, on "The Depression in the Cotton Trade," will observe that there is a small variation in the figures given in this treatise, as compared with those given in the pamphlet referred to. The amount expended in intoxicating liquors is here put down as greater—which, as has been explained, arises from taking higher estimates as to the selling prices of liquor. It will be observed also, that the value of the home consumption of cotton goods is estimated at a higher figure. The calculation was originally made out, as a comparison between the cotton goods exported and the cotton goods used at home, and was based (correctly enough) upon the cotton consumed for each; but, in estimating the values, the calculation was based upon the value of the goods—that is cloth—exported, instead of taking the value both of goods and yarns. This error in no way affected the figures given as to the falling off in the quantities of the home trade, but it made the estimate as to the expenditure somewhat too low.

Printed by John Heywood, Excelsior Works, Hulme Hall Road, Manchester.

www.ingramcontent.com/pod-product-compliance
Lightning Source LLC
Chambersburg PA
CBHW030245170426
43202CB00009B/632